The Beauty of Racism

The Beauty of Racism

Examining America's Hidden Caste System

AZIZ BEY

ISBN: 0692909168
ISBN 13: 9780692909164
Library of Congress Control Number: 2017909788
The Beauty of Racism, Bellflower, CA

In loving memory of
My father, Cordell Wilder, who showed me what
it truly means to be a family man, and
My hero, Kahlief Browder, a true warrior for truth and right, a martyr.

Contents

Salutations

FIRST AND FOREMOST, I must thank Allah SWT for making me Mu'Min (a believer) and blessing me with the faculties of reading, writing, and overstanding. Without such blessings, none of this is even remotely possible.

I would also like to extend heartfelt thanks and blessings to all of those who have made the decision to stand for truth and right. And especially to those among us who have continued this fight against an oppressive system of subjugation that is called *global white supremacy.*

This system as we currently know it is protected by white or European racism twenty-four hours a day, 365 days a year.

The simple fact is that racism in America never sleeps or slumbers, and it never takes a day off.

In the words of our courageous Elder who crossed over to take her place alongside the Ancient Ones in this struggle, Dr. Frances Cress Welsing, "Racism is a verb, meaning it is always in action."

To my forefathers, it is your magnificent energy and passionate struggle against the very system that fuels generations, like me, to pick up the fight and continue forward.

Although our ancestors' struggle was honorable and valiant, it did not end racism; therefore, I truly believe this fight is really just beginning.

I would also like to specifically highlight and mention some very dear people in my life who I feel have played a major role in the creation of this book and who are also partly responsible for inspiring me to become a better Muslim, Muur, father, friend, and husband.

To my wonderful family, I would like thank you for the love as well as your patience in putting up with me, especially during some of my most trying times.

To my beautiful children—Dcarri, Malachi, and my chocolate drop, better known as Mykae—I truly hope that this compilation of my thoughts displayed in book form makes you proud!

To my beautiful wife, Tanganyika, although at times you may have questioned my approach to a certain topic, or I may have started a silly argument, through it all, you have remained loyal and have loved me for me while supporting my personal endeavors at the same time.

I know I am not the easiest man to love, but you do it with a level of grace and compassion. It is for that reason as well as others that I will always love you.

You are my empress, and I am your king man. I thank you for everything. Without your support, this book project would not be possible.

To my incredible circle of loved ones, Alim Muhammad El, B. J. Abron El, Hamid Bey, the Honorable Jah Prophet Hobsoni (Father), Empress Sharon, and Empress Ahnu, the entire House of Rastafari, and the Muur American community in Los Angeles and at large, I respectfully thank you for your friendship and guidance. In some of my most difficult times, you guys have remained steadfast, and for that, I will always love you!

So as the Bible states, "Iron sharpens Iron as Man sharpens Man." It has been through many years of studying and sharpening my mental blade at the Round Table or building with Alim El (words cannot explain, brother), that I feel it's time to share the teachings and findings with the world—but in particular my community.

Please Read!

I F YOU HAVE picked this book up and begun reading it, you most likely possess within yourself a sense of pride. And having pride in self and culture is not wrong at all; it makes one a lover of self. No, this is not vanity or arrogance I speak of but simply loving you, which is a very important aspect that appears to be lacking in our community.

Some of you may be reading this and asking, "Why?"

Because loving yourself allows you to love others as well as nature. When we love nature, we do so while thoroughly appreciating her bounty, which surrounds and supports us. When that is done, it also brings about a sense of balance that manifests on all planes.

This is accomplished when you are in tune with yourself and your surroundings. While being in tune, you probably have come to the realization that there are some serious problems facing us here in the good ole United States of America.

We have come to know this black cloud that constantly hovers over our community's head as *racism*. Many people with melanin or carbon know this cloud very well.

We know it so well that it appears to be growing darker and more menacing by the hour. Yes, racism is getting worse, and the only people who seem to believe that racism is indeed getting worse are those who feel the sting of it on a daily basis.

We happen to live in a society where if the issue of racial discrimination does not affect you and your kind personally, then the issue is pretty much nonexistent. After all, racism and bigotry had no real effect on the so-called white community in America, so in the heart and mind of the average pale-skin, racism is seen as a nonexistent topic. The let's-all-move-on attitude quickly becomes the norm.

Some may ask, how I can possibly say that racism is getting worse when we've had a black president at the helm of the United States of America.

That coupled with countless CEOs of color, who are leading or have led multimillion-dollar European corporations and who all appear to be doing quite well.

Individually.

For what it's worth, I think black people can now recognize the token black-hire tactic for the ruse it truly is—a ploy that is visually pleasing to the uninformed masses and used to give them the appearance that real tangible change has taken place in their respective communities.

But instead, the entire black community as a whole is in far worse condition than it was just a little over fifty years ago. The so-called black community in America has unknowingly and knowingly accepted the Europeans' culture with disastrous consequences. An example is the European version of Christianity, which at one time you fought *not* to have and you will now die before giving back.

The pale-skins' slave brands—like *black* and *African American*—you wear boldly and proudly as if you don't know who you really and truly are. It is sad, but a large majority of the black community truly does not know who they really are.

Woefully this is all by design.

The misnamed black man of America has fought in every illegal war instigated by his European counterpart. The so-called Negroes would even appear pleased to fight their wars; some would even go as far to complain of racism when they couldn't!

All the while, they support the Europeans' bogus claims of fighting to free a faraway people. Yet that same black man continues to experience blatant racism in *his very own* homeland.

This fighting, of course, was done in an effort to see that if black men killed for Europeans and for their cause, would the European then accept and respect them as men. That attempt has failed miserably, and the state of today's military veterans, regardless of ethnicity, can attest to that sobering fact.

If you're reading this book, you have come to the realization that the countless civil rights marches, protests, riots, and rallies; the starting and signing of petitions; and the entertaining of the European masses have not done one single thing to remove this black cloud called racism from above our heads, which, by the way, looks like it will remain positioned there for years to come.

That's if we do not act now.

For the misguided and misled black people of America who blindly celebrate the European's dream of freedom every July 4, this is done by joyously participating in festivities that include the consumption of pork, drinking of alcoholic beverages, and the lighting of fireworks.

These celebrations by black people take place—mind you, while their very own freedom eludes them—as if it's still 1776. Only this time it is 2017 and counting.

Every Sunday morning a large majority of the black community will be in church or wanting to be in church to glorify the slave masters' religious creed of Christianity. You know the one the slave masters violently imposed on you for the sole purpose of control-ling their newly acquired property.

And through it all, this black cloud of racism remains, although the black community has done everything to fit in and everything to assimilate into the white American society.

That attempt has failed horribly.

Can it be because equal assimilation was never really a part of the pale-skins' plan to begin with?

This system of racism is so entrenched and ingrained in our society that I would often say that if our society was a blanket, then racism would be the thread that binds and holds it all together. In short, I guess what I'm saying is that I believe that European rac-ism is in every aspect and institution in American society.

If you're reading this book, then it's likely that you have some serious questions and concerns regarding our community here as well as our status internationally.

I did not start this project thinking that this manuscript alone would end global white supremacy.

No, that thought truly never entered my mind-set.

It is my hope that this book will generate a much-needed and refreshed approach to this long-standing dilemma. It is as simple as that. No other motive is necessary.

This system of maltreatment is constantly changing and adjust-ing to confront any new threats it may perceive to its power. When we couple our problems with the emergence of the information age, shouldn't the black community, at the very least, consider updating and rethinking its approach to this order of chaos we know as racism?

I am of the humble opinion—and the melaninated people of North America should all be in agreement with this as well—that the approach of our community to racism has, thus far, been, at the very least, tragically ineffective.

What is this affliction we know as racism?

It has been passed on from generation to generation and from one time period to the next. Yet here we are in the twenty-first century, discussing the ever-increasing problem of discrimination!

Again, how is this so?

I think I may have some information to shed some light on this topic as well as others, and I would love to share it with you. Let us begin.

Introduction

Insight

The people will only organize and unite
when their conditions change.

—MARCUS GARVEY

As a youth growing up in crime-infested South Central Los Angeles, which also happens to be the gang capital of the entire globe, I noticed the deplorable conditions that will, in fact, numb you over time. So I just came to accept what my neighborhood was and figured that everyone grew up as I did.

It wasn't until years later that I realized how wrong I was.

But instead of being consumed with what was taking place in my own community, I found myself asking questions of my mother concerning the system of South African apartheid. I was deeply moved by their struggle for freedom, and at that time, I was between twelve and fifteen years old.

That was a little odd—maybe—but now I have a clearer over-standing as to why I was concerned about things that a normal child my age and from my environment would not normally be worried about.

I am also of the belief that certain things happen in our lives that prepare us for whatever path we choose to follow.

It was Mark Twain (yeah, I know Mark Twain!) who stated, "The two most important days in your life are when you're born and when you realize what you're born for."

For a person who possesses melanin in this country, the mere possession of said melanin can be very dangerous. We are at a time in our society when a twenty-year-old black male can get seventy years in prison for credit-card fraud, while the Wall Street criminals and bankers who caused the economic collapse of 2008 remain free and clear of any charges.

It was during the economic collapse of 2008 that millions of homes were lost and countless families were destroyed, many of the victims committing suicide because the stress of the financial downturn was too much to bear. All the while, the justice department deemed that the banks and their fellow Wall Street crime cronies were too big to jail.

Although I do not know the particulars of the young brother's case, I do know that it pales in comparison to what the criminals on Wall Street have done and continue to do to this very day.

The two glaring differences in both circumstances are that one has melanin and very little monetary resources, and the other doesn't have melanin and has access to unlimited monetary resources, resources that he or she freely donates to political campaigns, thus ensuring that his or her crimes remain hidden and that he or she, the perpetrator, never sees the inside of a prison cell.

See, one of the main problems that I have with capitalism is that, at some point, everything—including politicians—has a price. It is also why I have come to believe that a government can have capitalism or democracy, but it cannot have both. It will eventually lead directly to what is taking place in this country right now, and that is called an *oligarchy*.

Please do not be fooled by their use of words like *lobbying* and *campaign finance*; it is really just an attempt to make bribery legal.

The so-called black community as a whole in America is in a very sad state right now, and much of this can be traced back directly to the early contact with European nationals. We can no longer believe the song by the talented and deceased singer Sam Cook, "A change is gonna come."

If so, I humbly ask, when?

How can a people's situation change when there is no change in the people? How can we expect things to be different in our dealings with the issue of race in America when we always approach the same problem with the very same solution? When we do this over and over again all the while expecting a different result?

It was Albert Einstein who defined insanity as "doing the same thing over and over again while expecting different results." According to our inaction or *passive* technique in handling this racial problem in America and the above quote, we, as a community and a society, are insane.

Our insanity relates to us finding a solution for this ever-growing issue of simply living in harmony together with those of different ethnic groups—an idea that seems to escape much of white America.

No, those in the black community are not an insane people. But they are a spoiled people when it comes to seriously confronting what we know the problem to be: global white supremacy.

This is a brutal system of oppression based entirely on violence and deceit. Scholar and historian Kaba Kamene said, "If black folk want to deal with their problems and they are not dealing with global white supremacy, then they are not dealing with their problems!"

Racism, by definition, means the notion that one's own ethnic stock is superior to someone else's. A *bigot* is defined as one who is *fanatically* devoted to one's own group, religion, race, or politics and intolerant of those who differ.

Racism, per the definition, involves the oppression of an entire race based on the notion that your very own ethnic stock is better, hence the word *race* in racism. Bigotry is an entirely different matter; it deals with the individual, not the race, which is a huge difference.

Racism and the conquering of a people cannot be accomplished without some form of institutional power structure in place. It can be done through the use of the military, law, and economics, but there has to be government or *corporations* or agencies in place in order to oppress the desired ethnic group.

It is the European nationals who are oppressing people of color here and abroad, and they are doing it for—at least in their minds—their own earthly well-being and survival.

We must, as a people, begin realize this fact.

Our community truly underestimates the lengths and the depths to which the pale-skin nations will go to oppress melaninated people for their very own survival. When we overstand this, our situation regarding our community, our race, and our *national* status becomes much clearer.

It was the honorable Dr. Martin Luther King Jr. who called militarism, racism, and economic exploitation—or capitalism—the "giant triplets" of European oppression. On April 4, 1967, he said, "We as a nation must undergo a radical revolution of values…When machines and computers, profit motives and property rights, are considered more important than people; the giant triplets of racism, extreme materialism, and militarism are incapable of being conquered."[2]

While I most certainly agree with our elder, I would also like to expound on his statement and update it for our generations' needs. It was after many years of experiencing racism personally and researching Dr. Martin Luther King's speech that I've come to the following conclusion.

Racism is the desired protector of global white supremacy, and it can be easily identified by five categories or, as I like to say, *pillars*. Try to imagine for a second that if racism was a house or a building, then it would most surely be supported by these five columns:

1. Capitalism
2. Religion
3. Law (civil law)
4. Entertainment
5. Violence (police/military)

These are the tools of oppression, and they are actively being waged against our community for the earthly survival of the European nation.

In the following chapters, we will attempt to take a very detailed glimpse into capitalism, religion, law, entertainment, and violence. We will explore how these tools are used by the ruling European powers to keep the so-called blacks of North America

---

2 Beyond Vietnam: A Time To Break Silence, Riverside Church, New York, April 15th, 1967

mentally, spiritually, and economically enslaved. The topic of *nationality* will be discussed in greater detail as well, as I will try to bring about some clarity to our overstanding of this long-standing conflict.

Yes, it is conflict, and some will even go as far as to say it is a war—a war that has the European plotting a deadly end. This deadly end has been kept secret, and for that reason, much of our community has yet to be aware of this plan. Those who are aware have taken secret oaths to conceal what I believe is causing us great damage as a community.

With all that being said, here's the Michael Jackson twist! (Peace, MJ.) What if this thing called racism is just *another* smoke screen or a diversion, a magic trick of sorts?

You know how the magicians get you to focus on the left hand when the real business or action is taken place in the right hand? What if this is one giant ploy to get you focused on what the European wants?

And to not focus on these things may actually help remove the so-called black man and woman from under the thumb of European jurisdiction, which is nationality and status. For those who may be a bit surprised, yes, black people have a nationality, and nationality just happens to determine an individual's political status in any given society.

Everyone on the planet has one; it comes from the word *natural* or *nature*, meaning land.

The topic of nationality is very interesting, and it may explain why one can hear crickets or, as my dad would say, it would be "so quiet you can hear a rat pissing on cotton!" That is the deafening silence one hears when the subject of African Americans and nationality is brought up—if it is brought up at all.

How many of you have ever heard those two words in conjunction with each other? I and many others like me know why you haven't, and it is crucial that you know as well.

For starters, we know from the definition of the word *black* that it is an *adjective* that describes a *noun*. If that is true—and it is— then the question becomes, what is your noun?

Asking a person "What is your noun?" is just the same as asking "Who are you?" On a more important note, can someone or something just take your nationality from you?

Let us consider, for an instant, that your nationality is your first and true identification that comes from your creator. So how can someone come and take away another person's nationality?

Many black people in the general public have been tricked into believing all types of things, such as the idea that black is a race or nationality, when it is not. It is that mentality that was the precursor of the three-fifths slave-tax clause that is written into the US Constitution, and, yes, of course we will cover this in greater detail as well.

If you are a black person and for some reason you do not believe that there are a handful of very old and ultra-wealthy families that are also deeply involved in secret societies, and that these secret societies are actively concealing information about your true history and status, you, my friend, are sadly mistaken.

For those of you who may be wondering why I say "so-called" black people when I mention individuals from the so-called African American community, it is because those two labels are brands that denote corporate property and not nationalities.

The concept comes from cattle branding.

Only, in this case, it is human cargo requiring labeling so one can travel the world and see all of its wondrous glory. But if you're traveling while wearing one of these brands—black or African American—that label is simply letting the host country know that you are property of the corporate organization called the United States of America.

This is the much-needed discussion that I and others as well, feel us as a community should be having. It is the hope of this writer that this book will spark that much-needed discussion.

In any criminal investigation, it is the experts themselves who say, "It is always best to follow the money," so let us begin with the first pillar of racism: capitalism.

1

Capitalism

*Let me issue and control a nation's money
and I care not who makes its laws.*

—Mayer Amschel Rothschild (1744–1812), founder
of the House of Rothschild banking dynasty

To begin this chapter, we must first define exactly what money is and how it ended up enslaving much of humanity, in particular the African American community. The US dollar is a promissory note, debt instrument, or debt note. It is a promise to pay a debt sometime in the near future.

At one time, the dollar was backed by gold, but it was President Franklin Delano Roosevelt who, in 1933, committed treason and removed the US form of currency called the dollar from the gold standard. More importantly, the privately owned Federal Reserve stopped redeeming dollars with gold. This was done by President Richard Nixon in 1971.

According to *Black's Laws* and *Webster's Dictionary*, "Banknotes are promissory notes," which is evidence of debt.[2] Banknotes issued after October 27, 1977, are "null and void."[3]

So, by definition, the dollar isn't even real money, yet we need it for every aspect of our daily lives. The basic needs our creator gave us—food, water, clothing, and shelter—are now for sale. And the only way to do this transaction in our society is by using the dollar or debt notes.

Then when you add in the materialism factor (the need to purchase things you really don't need), the enslavement to the dollar only worsens. The outcome is usually harmful to society as well as nature, but it strengthens those who seek to exploit humanity's servitude to this fiat currency.

Let us revisit that quote, by Mr. Rothschild, at the beginning this chapter. His family owns the largest and wealthiest banking dynasty humanity has ever seen. His family is also part owner of the *privately* operated Federal Reserve Bank, which, mind you, prints the dollar out of thin air and then charges you interest on it.

If I own something that you and much of society need for your very survival and sustenance, wouldn't that make me and those closely associated with me very powerful?

I mean, talk about leverage.

As Muammar Gaddafi said, "Man's freedom is lacking if somebody else controls what he needs; this results in man's enslavement of man."

It was the Rothschild family who funded both sides of the Civil War and then funded the Reconstruction of this "new" country.

---

2 See *US Codes of the Law*, Title 12, sections 561 3754.
3 See *US Codes of Law*, Title 31, section 511(d)(1)(2).

History has shown us that countries tend to get destroyed when bombs start falling. This diabolical theme will repeat itself in the many wars to come in the near future.

All wars are started by international bankers by way of the money lent to governments to wage war.

These loans were given to the US government, with interest of course, to fund this rebuilding project, and later the pale-skins needed workers or slaves with skills to build this new nation. See, the building of this new nation required the European to be skillful in other tasks besides killing and enslaving.

It was the pale-skin who needed slaves or workers.

Slaves didn't just pick cotton and pour ice-cold lemonade for their massas. No, that was not the case at all; these slaves were the only skilled tradespeople in the country at that time.

I will attempt to explain the Atlantic slave trade in greater detail and with a commonsense approach, because one cannot properly discuss the so-called slave story without addressing true ancient history. And when one is discussing true, ancient history, one cannot leave out the Africans/Muurs.

Any attempt to do so would be comparable to doing math without the use of numbers zero to nine. It's not even remotely possible. You just can't do it.

Now this ability to print money literally out of thin air and then to charge interest gave the Rothschild as well as other European families enormous power and influence to go along with tremendous wealth.

The Rothschild banking dynasty, who are of European descent—along with twelve other American and European families—comprises what is known as the Illuminati. What you have, in my view, are families who are ultra-wealthy and just happen to worship an evil force or spirit, while referring to themselves as Luciferians.

As an example of the Rothschild's vast wealth, I once read that an elder member of the family passed his physical form, and upon his death, it was found that one of his many bank accounts had over *$17 trillion* in it. I don't know how true the story is, but I do know that saying that the Rothschild is rich and/or wealthy is a gross understatement.

The Rothschild banking dynasty initially made its fortune laundering the resources and gold stolen from the Saracens, or Muurs, by the Roman Catholic Church. That made them a pretty penny to say the least, which allowed them to become a very powerful and immeasurable entity that still exists to this very day.

The Roman Catholic Church, on the other hand, had to be feeling supremely arrogant when they wrote what was to become the *casus belli*, or case for war. This war was to be fought against the melaninated Muurs of the newly discovered America(s). To be straightforward, it was this case for war that instructed the European Christian nations to kill and/or enslave the Saracens, another word for Muurs, and steal their earthly possessions and lands.

Contrary to popular belief, the Roman Empire did not dissolve or just go away. No, it moved west violently—to the Americas. In today's military terminology, Christopher Columbus would be a scout or a pathfinder. Scouts are soldiers as well, but their main job is to tell the larger fighting force (the Spanish military) what to expect—like how many people there are, if there is gold, and if the people can be defeated and then enslaved.

So Mr. Columbus did, in fact, discover the Americas. He discovered it for European conquest and exploitation.

Let's say that I owned a company or corporation and I forced or tricked people into free labor, and I did this for hundreds of years. Wouldn't that company have a leg up in the profit margin?

It wasn't like these plantation owners were paying wages and benefits. Comprehending that fact alone, one can overstand how this newly formed country called the United States of America got so wealthy, so fast.

One very important factor we must overstand is that when this new government failed to repay the loans to the international bankers or the Rothschild banking dynasty, it ceased being a sovereign and free republic.

It became a federal democratic corporation.

By law, all corporations have to make money by any means necessary. Again I ask you, whose law?

I am attempting to set the stage so that the reader can overstand that slavery was not just a mere part of the US economy. It *was* the US economy, and when we get into the next chapter, the reader will see that the practice of slavery still exists today.

The sadistic use of slavery made certain Europeans in America very rich, and their government would later go on to become one of the wealthiest nations on the planet for years to come.

Because black bodies were producing cotton, sugar, tobacco, coffee, and cocoa, which were in such high demand, it gave European corporations a serious economic advantage.

This marriage of sorts put the US and European corporations in a pretty successful position on the global market, particularly those in the south where slavery was making plantation owners enormous wealth due, in large part, to the rise of the agriculture industry.

The Muur/African slave trade also galvanized European shipping, manufacturing, and gun-making markets. European industries—such as shipbuilding, farming, and fishing—also profited greatly from slavery.

It was through this uncontrollable drive for capital gains and control that the Europeans became wealthy on the backs of the recently defeated Muurs of the Muur Empire, who would become denationalized and forced into slavery.

Thus the foundation of this capitalist system was laid for generations to come. This vicious use of forced servitude made the common European in America—the plantation owner—very rich and the international bankers even wealthier. It was slavery that stimulated the US banking and insurance industries as well as iron, textiles, and rum making.

The economic destruction of the Muurs was, and continues to be, a win-win for the pale-skin nation. But it was a horrible loss for those who were enslaved, and quite frankly our people have never rebounded from that crushing defeat.

In an unmatched display of what I call *delusional arrogance*, in this, the year of 2017, the so-called white community still downplays the financial jackpot slavery was for Europeans in the newly formed US colonies. Acknowledging this fact would then force the white community to make the connection between slavery and today's economic disparities that exist between the white and black communities.

One is drastically gaining wealth, while the other is losing what little wealth it never really had. That's because true wealth is in the land. The Europeans overstand this concept wholeheartedly, and all their stolen income comes from the bounty of nature.

This manipulation of wealth and land by the pale-skins enabled them to put laws in place barring black people from owning and/or purchasing property and/or land. These Roman laws, which are put in place after the land is stolen, are something that I find quite interesting.

Those who committed the initial crime then get to make laws to cover their crime, all while depriving the victim of any form of reparation. This process is still going on today, with what now is called economic and neighborhood gentrification, or, as I like to call it, *economic apartheid*.

How it works is pretty simple. The rich European nationals, or white people, identify their neighborhood of choice. Then they revamp the location and set the property price very high so that only a select economic bracket, can afford to live there. This process largely excludes people of color, especially blacks.

The economic vibration of years of exploitation is still being felt throughout our community today. The effects can be seen in today's society all around us.

People—specially people of color—are not committing crimes because they are rich and have nothing better to do with their time other than to rob or steal! No, they are poor and hungry. They want to eat, and their children are poor and hungry and want to eat, too!

How many lives have been lost and families destroyed for a promissory debt note?

We all know that there is a direct correlation between an individual's educational and economic status and crimes being committed. Only now, with the outgrowth of the private-prison industry, anything that can be made to resemble a crime is of monetary profit for European private-prison corporations in America.

Last time I checked, products at Starbucks, Target, Victoria's Secret and just about all office furniture are made in private prisons by prisoners who just happened to be branded black, Latino and white.

And they are branded as such because a large majority of the prison population does not know who they are. So when you don't know yourself, you readily accept names or brands from anyone.

This includes brands from your known oppressor.

The ruling European nations overstood early on that capitalism could be used as a weapon against the melaninated people of the America(s) while simultaneously being a great resource for their own community.

Take, for instance, this card-playing analogy used by the American political scientist Roy L. Brooks almost two decades ago. It goes as follows:

> Two persons—one white and the other black—are playing a game of poker. This game has been in progress for some three hundred years. One player—the white one—has been cheating during much of this time, but now announces, "From this day forward, there will be a new game and with new players and no more cheating."
>
> Hopeful but suspicious, the black player responds, "That's great.
>
> "I've been waiting to hear you say that for three hundred years.
>
> "Let me ask you, what are you going to do with all those poker chips that you stacked up on your side of the table all these years?"
>
> "Well," said the white player, somewhat bewildered by the question, "they are going to stay right here of course."
>
> "That's unfair," snaps the black player. "The new white player will benefit from your past cheating. Where's the equality in that?"

"But you can't realistically expect me to redistribute the poker chips along racial lines when we are trying to move away from considerations of race and when the future offers no guarantee to anyone," insists the white player.

"And surely," he continues, "redistributing the poker chips would punish individuals for something they did not do. Punish me, not the innocents!"

Emotionally exhausted, the black player answers, "But the innocents will reap a financial windfall."[4]

We can now bear witness that slavery *was* a brutal form of subjugation directed at the black people of the Americas, while, on the flipside, it made white America a financial powerhouse, and they continue to reap huge economic benefits to this very day.

This, of course, was and is all by design.

I sincerely hope this will begin to explain why black people are last in just about every economic category here and abroad.

Many people—including myself—argue that capitalism is horrible for the planet because it forces the earth's populace to consume more and more; instead of getting from nature what you and your family need for your sustenance.

You now have large mega corporations that again—by law—have to make a fiscal profit, at any cost. In this unquenchable push to make money, those who are leading this push are literally destroying our planet in the process.

My question again is whose law?

Are there not laws to protect the environment? Yes, I am sure there are such laws on the books, but there is also money

---

4 Paul Street, False Flag Change: History, the Confederate Flag, Obama and the Deeper American Racism, Counterpunch.org, July 10th, 2015.

involved, which will be used pay the so-called lawmakers off and continue with business.

Remember this chapter's opening quote...

Let me issue and control a nation's money
and I care not who makes its laws.

—MAYER AMSCHEL ROTHSCHILD *(1744–1812),* FOUNDER
OF THE HOUSE OF ROTHSCHILD BANKING DYNASTY

Capitalism and greed stifle technologies that would otherwise truly benefit the earth and her earthlings. Any new invention that is beneficial to humanity is quickly deemed a threat to capitalism and is either bought out or the product plus the inventor are never seen again.

Take, for example, the story of probably one of the greatest—if not *the* greatest—inventors of all time, in my opinion, Nikola Tesla. He was hailed as one of the greatest geniuses of his day. It was his proving of scalar energy that propelled his ideas years ahead of his peers.

Based on energy secrets dating back to ancient Ta'Muure, which has been falsely labeled Egypt, Mr. Tesla referred to his findings as scalar energy technology.

As a matter of note, so-called black people, anytime you're reading anything and it mentions the word *ancient*, pay very close attention.

Now back to Mr. Tesla. He had a theory, and proved it—that he could provide limitless and wireless free energy to everybody, which was amazing in the 1940s. What noble a gesture!

The problem with his research was that it was being funded by J. P. Morgan, of the American banking dynasty, who also owned and supplied much of the copper wire that was being used to bring electricity to many homes and businesses throughout the continental United States.

This family, along with eleven others, makes up your so-called Illuminati.

So Mr. J. P. Morgan understood the enormous financial ramifications if Mr. Tesla's invention of limitless and wireless power made it to market and then to the consumer.

It is said that J. P. Morgan forced Nikola Tesla to sell the technology. It is said that J. P. Morgan used the media, of which he owned a large majority percentage, to publicly discredit Nikola Tesla, thus ensuring that his invention never saw the light of day.

Can you begin to imagine a world with free energy? Incredibly, Mr. Tesla's work was confiscated, and neither he nor his work was ever seen again, which of course is truly sad.

How about a technology that would allow cars to run a one hundred miles per gallon on regular, ole water? Mr. Stan Meyer achieved this feat and said that his technology was going to market—for the public. He said this after refusing many lucrative offers to sell his invention to the government and, of course, to the oil industry.

But before he could fulfill his dream—according to his autopsy report and Mr. Meyer's last words to his brother—he was poisoned to death after a meeting with government officials. His invention and his partners went underground. And like Mr. Tesla, his work was never to be seen or heard of again.

When comedian Chris Rock went on stage and said, "There is no profit in the cure," ones&ones (so-called black people) laughed, and rightfully so. It was hilarious, but it was also tragically true.

These huge pharmaceutical companies and the medical industry conspire with the FDA to actively block or discredit anything in relation to natural cures for any disease.

Much of the world—including the US government—knows the herb that is currently misnamed *marijuana, which is* a slang that has no meaning. It is misnamed and mislabeled because the herb is also a natural cure for cancer, diabetes, asthma, and post-traumatic stress disorder, commonly called PTSD, and many other medical ailments.

Now what is truly special about this plant is that everything described in the above paragraph comes from the male seed. See, there are two seeds: male and female. The female seed is what is smoked, and the male seed is used for countless other purposes, up to and including manufacturing wood—made from hemp, which is ten times stronger than that of trees, saving much-needed trees for the environment—paper, biofuel, clothes, shoes, soap, teas, and butter!

The herb is also packed with natural cancer-fighting qualities. And since one liar and cheat by the name of Lance Armstrong raised $500 million by himself for cancer research, one can clearly see that the cancer industry in the United States is a multibillion-dollar business.

It appears that when anything threatens a European corporation in America, the government, which is a corporation itself, is always there to protect the "interests" of the private corporation.

This is done at any and all costs.

The desired goal is having private European corporations running the lives of ordinary citizens. That plan is to be supported by the use of violence.

Now once the US government is deployed overseas, its paid mouthpieces tell the unassuming fluoride-consuming American public that they are going overseas to fight for freedom and democracy when in reality they are in foreign lands fighting for corporate profit and control.

To bring this chapter to a close, I would like to end with an excerpt from a speech given by Major General Smedley Butler of the United States Marine Corps., in 1933. He said,

> I spent most of my time being a high-class muscle-man for Big Business, for Wall Street and for the Bankers. In short, I was a racketeer, a gangster for capitalism...I helped make Mexico, especially Tampico, safe for American (European) oil interests in 1914. I helped make Haiti and Cuba a decent place for the National City Bank boys to collect revenue in. I helped in the raping of half a dozen Central American republics for the benefits of Wall Street. I helped purify Nicaragua for the international banking house of Brown Brothers in 1909–1912. I brought light to the Dominican Republic for American sugar interests in 1916. In China I helped to see to it that Standard Oil went its way unmolested.[5]

---

5 General Smedley Butler, USMC, Speaking Tour, War Is A Racket, 1930.

2

Law

Ignorance of the law excuses no man.

—JOHN SELDON (1584–1654)

IT WAS A beautiful, sunny day in South Central Los Angeles, so I decided to go for a little drive. I hopped in my transport, or car, and proceeded to travel west on Manchester Boulevard.

While playing my music—not loudly—as I crossed Main Street right near the 110 freeway, I noticed an unmarked LAPD vehicle with two occupants inside. The car was going in the opposite direction.

The driver was black, and I guess his partner was of Latino descent. Both stared at me rather aggressively as we slowly passed one another in opposing traffic.

Since I had committed no crime and was not "riding dirty," I felt pretty comfortable that I would not have any interaction with the police!

Boy, how wrong I was.

The police, who were traveling east on Manchester, did an abrupt U-turn and were now following me. For people with melanin in this country, this is not a sight we like to see.

I could literally fell the stress build in my body.

I knew from the way the driver executed that U-turn and by the way he got behind me that they were going to pull me over, but I was also well aware of the fact that I had to remain calm.

I had to because out of everyone in the continental United States, my chances of getting beaten by the Popo (what we call police, but I personally like the other name: *roman soldiers*) or getting a bullet placed in my skull that kills me increase as my skin tone gets darker.

This is an established fact. The police officer gets a two-week paid vacation or administrative leave and then returns to his or her police duties, probably with accolades. Life goes on for the officer as if nothing ever happened!

Now, as I said before, I knew by the sudden U-turn that they were going to pull me over.

And they did just that. So now I was hit with lights. I was pulled over, and at this point, I was not thinking about what they pulled me over for. I'm thinking, *Please, Allah SWT, let me get out of this unscathed and with life.*

My own!

So I pulled over into a parking lot, and the police did also. They were now approaching my transport from both sides—passenger and driver. I was then instructed to get out of the vehicle, which I did, very cautiously, very cognizant about not making any sudden movements at all.

The funny thing, though, is that with all their weaponry and police training (it's well over $100,000 to train one cop for LAPD), they always seem to be rather scared of unarmed and untrained black people.

The police then handcuffed me for no apparent reason at all. I mean, I was unarmed, and at this point, I was still praying for my own safety.

They never gave me any reason for stopping me or placing me in handcuffs, nor did they feel that they had to. Now, to be fair, the police officers were respectful and polite, but polite cops kill unarmed, respectful black people all the time.

As for their very courteous law-enforcement work, it did not make me feel very safe at all.

See, I am well aware of the police force's history of systemic abuse, and that alone prevailed over my encounter with the polite police officers. But through the entire ordeal, what really made me uncomfortable was being placed in handcuffs and made to sit on the street curb as if I were a common criminal.

This embarrassed and infuriated me!

Because now I was sitting on the ground, in the middle of the day, with handcuffs on my wrists, for no apparent reason whatsoever.

And although I was eventually released without incident or harm, the brush with LAPD's finest got me to thinking, where does the City of Los Angeles, a *corporation*, get the jurisdiction to do this to me, a live, spirit-filled human being?

How is this even possible?

How can an organization, like the city of Los Angeles, that exists only on paper have this much authority over my natural body?

If the police were just acting on brute force and intimidation, what good are these laws that the white community consistently brags about?

Then, as usual, my thoughts begin to race, and a flurry of other questions began to flood my mind, like how can Child Protective Services, another corporation, just come and take our children?

How is it that when it is done, the parent involved literally has no say in the matter?

Or how can these government entities, which are acting in unison with the pharmaceutical companies, force known harmful vaccinations on you and your child?

Or why are the working poor of this country duped and forced into giving up 40 percent of their hard-earned paychecks to the privately owned, debt-collection agency called the Internal Revenue Service?

Question: If you had a guest in your home, would you allow that guest to take over your home and then have you pay him or her rent and taxes and then subject you to his or her laws, all while he or she resides in your home?

Sometimes death is better than slavery.

It is one thing to be a slave in a foreign land, and yet it's an entirely different issue to be a slave on your own land. Because with land come resources, and with resources come capital, and with capital or the prospect of obtaining capital come problems—usually in the form of an invading foreign force, hell-bent on taking your resources for their capital gains.

For the money-worshipping people of American society, the pursuit of capital has literally become an obsession. This bizarre love affair exists; as every aspect of our life is either taxed or fined.

It has to make one wonder, though. Where does all of this money that has been collected in the form of taxes and traffic fines go? Where do the fees for getting a driver's license and registering your car go?

There's one place we know the fees for taxes and traffic fines don't go, and that is back into the infrastructure of the communities that house the predominantly poor black and Latino folk.

Karen Hudes, a Yale graduate, worked twenty years in the legal department for the World Bank. It was her investigation that uncovered the secret dealings of the international bankers and the Vatican who are definitely getting a cut of the average workers hard-earned income.

So, it may shock the reader to learn that 60 percent of your take-home income goes directly to the Roman Catholic Church or specifically the Vatican—a sovereign city of its own—free and clear of any government jurisdiction.

The other 40 percent goes to the international bankers, or the Rothschild banking dynasties, that are also part owners of the Federal Reserve and are located in Great Britain.

The Rothschild banking dynasty resides in a sovereign city known as the Crown, which, much like the Vatican, is free and clear of any state or governmental laws and jurisdiction. They remain unattached from any outside intrusion, largely because they outright own all Western governments.

The third sovereign city is one you might be very familiar with. It's called Washington, DC, and it, along with Great Britain, takes its orders from the Roman Catholic Church.

It is said that there are three corporations that run the entire world, and they are as follows: the Vatican, which calls the shots; the British crown, which runs the finances; and the United States of America, which does the trio's wet work or warmongering.

The corporate state of Washington, DC, only has jurisdiction within a ten-mile radius of the District of Columbia. Its jurisdiction only spreads to those individuals who contract with this corporation knowingly or unknowingly.

The abovementioned corporations are the triple-headed monster that represents global white supremacy.

Are we clear?

OK, let us now take a look at how this is possible and how it relates to our current situation here in America.

But first, I think it's vital that we cover some legal definitions that apply directly to our conditions here in America. We will also have a bit of a history lesson; this will help us put these events into proper perspective. I think—or shall, I say I know—that you're going to find this very interesting.

Let's begin with some definitions.

We must do this—and you will find that I will give definitions throughout the book—because ones&ones tend to use words and not truly know the legal meaning of them or the way that they affect their everyday lives.

A few of these are ordinary words that have dual meanings: a *regular* definition and a *legal* definition, two very different definitions for the same word. Let us begin with the word *nationality*.

Nationality determines the political status of the individual, especially with reference to allegiance, while domicile determines his civil status. Nationality arises either by birth or by naturalization.

Civiliter Mortuus means civilly dead, dead in the view of the law. It is the condition of one who has lost his or her civil rights and capacities and is, therefore, accounted dead in law.[6] It is not the death of the physical frame or a person's appearance; it describes a person(s) political or civil standing within a given society.

Color of law is appearance or semblance, without the substance of legal rights. It is misuse of power possessed by virtue of state law and made possible only because the wrongdoer is clothed with the authority of the state.[7]

---

6 See Rasor v. Rasor, 173 SC 365,175 S.E. 545.

7 See Title 42, USCA, section 1983, P-6.

Artificial, as opposed to natural, means created or produced by man.[8]

Corporation is an *artificial* person or legal entity created by or under the authority of the laws of the state.[9]

Person, by statue, means a firm, labor organization, partnership, association, *corporation*, legal representative, trustee, trustee in bankruptcy, or receiver.[10] Persons are corporations and municipalities within the meaning of Title 42, USCA, section 1983.[11]

Civil law is the system of law predominant on the European continent and of which a form is in force in Louisiana. It is historically influenced by the codes of ancient Rome. Please note that Roman, or European, law is not rooted in natural law.

Now that we have covered some definitions, let's continue...

One minute I was driving up the street—seat belt on, minding my own business—and then the next minute, I was stopped by LAPD and handcuffed for no apparent reason.

Again I ask how this is remotely possible.

And for those of you who have some serious questions regarding this legal system and the private-prison complex it supports, you need go no further than the Thirteenth Amendment of the US Constitution.

The Thirteenth Amendment reads as follows: "Neither slavery nor involuntary servitude, except as a punishment for crime whereof the party shall have been duly convicted, shall exist within the United States, or any PERSON subject to their jurisdiction."

---

8 See California Casualty Indemnity Exchange v. Industrial Accident Commission of California, 13 Cal. 2d 529,90P.2d 289.

9 See Deathmouth College v. Woodward, 17 US (4 Wheat.) 518, 636, 657, 4 L.Ed. 629.

10 See the National Labor Relations Acts, section 2(L).

11 See Monell v. New York City Department of Social Services, 436 US 658.98 S.Ct.2013,56 L.Es. 2d 611.

So there you have it.

Clearly according to the unconstitutional Thirteenth Amendment, *slavery* is an acceptable form of punishment when the "person" has been convicted of a crime. Is there any wonder now why so-called blacks and Latinos are being warehoused in prison cells while slaving for corporate profit?

You can now bear witness to the pitfalls of having your oppressor label or brand you!

The failure of the African American community to proclaim a *nationality* has, in turn, made them wards of the bankrupt, European, corporate state.

This is the meaning of *Civiliter Mortuus* or "dead in the eyes of the law" European law.

The European national is enforcing Roman law on Muur Land (America or Al Maghrib Al Aska) by way of deceit, fear, and fraudulent contracts. It clearly states in a US Supreme Court ruling that *corporations* can only interact or "contract" with other *corporations*.

In *Penhallow v. Doane's Administrators*, the Supreme Court stated,

> In as much as every government is an artificial person, an abstraction, and a creature of the mind only, a government can INTERFACE only with other artificial persons. The imaginary, having neither actuality nor substance, is foreclosed from creating and attaining parity with the tangible. The legal manifestation of this is no government; as well any law, agency, aspect, court, etc. can concern itself with anything other than corporate, artificial persons and the contracts between them.[12]

---

12 See SCR 1795, Penhallow v. Doane's Administrators, 3 US 54; 1 L.Ed. 57; 3 Dall. 54.

When the US republic at that time defaulted on its loans from the international bankers, it ceased being a sovereign, independent republic and became a bankrupt federal democratic corporation. Let's see what the United States' very own law makers have to say about this government bankruptcy.

On March 17, 1993, Representative James Traficant Jr. of Ohio addressed the House of Representatives and said this:

> Mr. Speaker, we are here now in chapter eleven. Members of Congress are official trustees presiding over the greatest reorganization of any bankrupt entity in world history, the US Government. We are setting forth hopefully a blueprint for our future. There are some who say it is a coroner's report that will lead to our demise.
>
> It is an established fact that the US Federal Government has been dissolved by the Emergency Banking ACT, March 9, 1933, 48 Stat. 1, Public Law 89-719; declared by President Roosevelt, being bankrupt and insolvent. H.J.R. 192, 73rd Congress, session June 5 1933—Joint Resolution To Suspend The Gold Standard and Abrogate Authority of the United States and the official capacities of all US Governmental Offices, and Departments and is further evidence that the US Federal Government exists today in name only.
>
> The receivers of the US Bankruptcy are the International Bankers, via the United Nations, the World Bank and the International Monetary Fund.[13]

The republic essentially became a *federal democratic corporation,* which is why the words *democratic* and *democracy* are nowhere to

13 D. Robinson, *Give Yourself Credit* (North Charleston, SC: CreateSpace Publishing, 2010), 173.

be found in their US Constitution. The United States of America is also defined as a religious *corporation* managed by the Queen Elizabeth and is now under the complete control of the Vatican.[14]

And now this newly formed *democratic corporation*, which is pretending to be a sovereign government, could not repay its debt. It illegally gave up the *physical labor* and *future work earnings* of its population—the US citizens, who have been incorporated themselves and are now classified as corporations.

This was done in secret and as collateral for the debt owed to the international bankers—mainly the European Rothschild banking dynasty. The question I feel should be asked now is, how is this remotely possible if corporations can only contract with corporations?

As Henry Ford, the founder of the Ford Motor Company, said, "It is well enough that people of the nation do not understand our banking and money system, for if they did, I believe there would be a revolution before tomorrow morning."

It is not my intention to fully explain the entire financial system, but a portion of it has to be revealed and included. Here's why.

We also know that the newly formed US republic owed a debt to the Rothschild banking dynasty of England. And since this new republic could not repay their debt, they defaulted on said loans and filed for bankruptcy, thus becoming a "federal democratic corporation" according to the Banking Act of 1871.

Before 1871, the original US Constitution read, "the United States for America." Now, after the Banking Act of 1871, the constitution reads, "the United States of America." The subtle change from *for* to *of* was not a minor grammatical error.

No. It was far from being that.

---

14 See (Bened.XIV., De Syn. Dioec, lib, ix., c. vii., n. Prati, 1844) (Syllabus, prop 28,29 44).

The United States of America is now represented by block capitals, and the word *for* was changed to the word *of, which* means to possess.

From that point forward, all government buildings, banks, and schools would now display the American banner with the gold frill on the edges. That frill around the flag symbolizes admiralty and maritime law or, simply put, *contract law.*

This is the reason why when you receive any mail from a government agency, at the federal, state, or local level, your name appears differently. Your name is in *all capitals* now, yet you may not have noticed the incorrect grammar in the usage of your name. That incorrect grammar is the spelling of your name in *all capital* letters.

For instance, when you receive a bill or a traffic ticket or get a letter from a debt-collection agency like the Internal Revenue Service, you should notice the spelling of your name, which of course really isn't your name, because it is always spelled in *all capitals.*

When your name is spelled in *all capitals* by the government, it means a *straw man* has been created as an imaginary, fake person for your real, natural body. So if your name is Seymour Money, and you get a letter from the city you live in for unpaid traffic tickets, your name would appear like this: "SEYMOUR MONEY."

So, Mr. SEYMOUR MONEY, you are getting this letter because we, the CITY OF PHILADELPHIA, a corporation, want to see more money from the natural, real, living, and breathing you.

What this truly means is this: you are now a corporation.

You are no longer a natural, spirit-filled being, who was once a child of The Most High, something you may have assumed you were before being made aware of this evil scheme. No. Now you are a man-made European subject, a fake entity, something deemed not real, chattel or, simply put, a slave.

The government can now deny you human rights while you foolishly beg for civil rights, *civil* meaning Roman or European rights, which of course are not possible for people with melanin.

Now the debt that the newly formed democratic corporation had is passed off to the states. Just about *all* the states of this union were incorporated under the bankrupted federal corporation, and they (the states), in turn, passed the debt off to its citizens.

That citizen will be you: the US citizen.

This mythical debt that the US government constantly speaks of has now been passed on to you and your children via the warehouse receipt now called a tax. The government that is really a corporation collects money for this debt in any way it chooses, but it is usually done in the form of what is known as an income tax.

Now with a natural spirit-filled person being made a corporation, it has also made you—the individual—a ward of the state through contracts your parents unknowingly entered you into with the state when you were born. And this is how the state can now pass this made-up debt on to you and your family just for the desired purpose of control.

As of now, it is my guess that the reader should be asking, what contract is this that the corporation called the United States of America uses to assume jurisdiction over my physical body? All of this treachery and scheming was done while hiding in plain sight—but only behind a corporate veil.

Please note that there are a total of four contracts that is very crucial you know about. Let us begin with the contract that got you into this corporate-status mess in the first place. It is called the certificate of live birth, commonly referred to now as the *birth certificate*.

First, let us define the term *contract*: a covenant or agreement between two or more persons, with a *lawful* consideration or cause. The contract that removed you from your natural state and made you a corporation is called a *birth certificate*.

We are well acquainted with the word *birth*, so let us define the word *certificate*. *Certificate* has two meanings we need to know:

- A written assurance, or official representation, that some act has or has not been done, that some event occurred, or that some legal formality has been complied with.
- A paper establishing an ownership claim. (Barron's *Dictionary of Banking Terms*)

Going by the above definitions of the word *certificate*, why is such a word assigned to a child's birth?

This corporation better known as the United States of America had to have a way of connecting your *real*, live, spirit-filled body to their *artificial*, bankrupt organization. This was done by what is called in the financial sector a *transmitting utility*.

A *transmitting utility* is defined as an agent used for the purpose of transmitting *commercial* activity for the benefit of the grantor or secured party. This is vital because this links the imaginary person—the Strawman—to the live, spirit-filled body—you.

The transmitting utility, or contract, that the government uses in this case is called the birth certificate. It is also a form of security commonly referred to as a *warehouse receipt*.

What our parents did was unknowingly sign us over to the bankrupt corporate state. When you take a closer look at the birth certificate, you will see that it lists the mother of the child as an *informant or one who gives information to another*. In this case, it was your birthright that was given to the criminal, bankrupt state who assumes that the baby is dead, not physically, and takes control over his or her trust or affairs.

This entire charade was only made possible through the highly treasonous Maternity Act, which made it mandatory that *all* live births be required to get a birth certificate. The birth certificate is then sent to the Children's Bureau of the US Department of Commerce and Labor, where it is placed as a registered security.

What this fraudulent contract called the birth certificate did was create a fictional entity represented by all caps, commonly known as a strawman. This man-made creation by the state was generated so that the *state*, a *corporation*—meaning not real—can contract with you and have jurisdiction over your real, live, spirit-filled body.

Webster's Ninth New Collegiate Dictionary defines the label *strawman* as the following:

1. A *weak* or *imaginary* opposition set up only to be easily confuted.
2. A *person* set up to serve as a cover for a usually *questionable* transaction.

Now for those of us, who may be in possession of our birth certificates, we will only see a copy; the state never relinquishes the original. The birth-certificate copy indicates a number of things. One of these is the red certificate number, which is reportedly openly traded on international stock markets.

It has also been reported that the Federal Reserve values each live birth between $600,000 and around $1 million. And since the states now have a registered live-birth document with the Department of Commerce, the government then uses that (contract) as collateral for this nonexistent debt.

This was done with the bogus intent of *you* repaying a loan that has nothing to do with Muurs, or black people, and everything to do with US citizens, or white people.

Why?

Because according to a New York Times magazine report and the US debt clock, *all US citizens are liable for $58,604 of the national debt per person.* The government, a corporation, is positioning itself to collect on this debt in any way it deems fit.

Remember: since there is no real money, there is no debt.

If this sounds like some sort of Ponzi scheme, that is because it is; the only real money that circulates in our society is the labor of the ill-informed US citizen. This is, hands down, the greatest fraud ever to have taken place in human history, and it is all backed by force.

Then to make it official, in the lower-left-hand corner of your birth certificate, where it says, "Any alteration or erasure voids this certificate," in the smallest of print—of course—it reads, "Midwest Banknote Company." It could go by any other name, but it will most certainly say, "Bank Note Company." The birth certificate is also written on special paper that is only used for financial transactions.

When your name appears in all caps, you are officially property of the corporation called the United States of America. See, slavery really never had an end. It just merely revised itself, and the only change that occurred was the ownership of said slaves. That ownership change was from the plantation individual to the newly formed, corporate state called the United States of America.

The birth certificate is very important not only because it made ones&ones a corporation, or Strawman, but also because it was part of a broader denationalization agenda.

To solidify this plan, they then added the totally unconstitutional and unnecessary Fourteenth Amendment. And from that point forward, the corporate state then proceeded to brand you *African American*—which, of course, replaced the previous brands, such as black (Negro), colored, and Ethiopian.

Isn't it interesting that you have been called every name under the sun by Europeans but never Muur/Moor, at least not since their violent conquest of the Americas?

So let us take a look at the Fourteenth Amendment of the US Constitution, which solidified the chattel brand we know as *African American*. Here is the Fourteenth Amendment of the US Constitution: "All persons born or naturalized in the United States, and subject to the jurisdiction thereof, are citizens of the United States; nor shall any state deprive any person within its jurisdiction the equal protection of the laws..."

The key word in this amendment is *persons*. Remember, legally the word *persons* is defined as a corporation, or simply not real.

A close friend once told me that you could look up your birth-certificate number on the financial-securities website called Fidelity. I tried, to no avail, but it would not surprise me one bit if this is at all possible. Although I was unable to look up my birth-certificate number, I personally believe it is being done.

I don't know. I guess one could call it a lack of trust in this system. Let us get back to the matter at hand: the birth certificate. If only our parents had known that anything in a contract that is not clearly defined before signing makes the contract null and void.

Let's recap. So when we were born, our parents unconsciously entered us into contracts with the corporate state. This one illegal act made the black community into *corporations* or *chattel property*, who are then ready to do business with other federal and corporate entities.

Now the state where you reside can interact with you as corporation to corporation, which also means that the state can apply *color of law* to all of its subjects—or those who are willing contract with it.

Remember the above definition of *color of law?*

The birth certificate is one of four contracts that this financially strapped government uses to assume jurisdiction over your body. This is what the definition of color of law meant when it said "clothed by the authority of the state." Get it?

These four fraudulent contracts are used to clothe and bind you to their corporate, European jurisdiction. This happens to be their deceitful form of jurisprudence called the color of law, which, to the untrained eye, looks like law, smells like law, but in reality it isn't law at all!

And with that being the case, the government's stance is basically this. Since you are now a corporation, you are now obligated to follow our (corporate) statutes and codes—not laws but *statutes* and *codes*—which are based in Roman or civil law and again are *not* rooted in natural law.

For instance, if you would like to start a business or simply operate a transport or a car, you must now get a business or driver's license to do so. When you do, you have just signed over your freedom of movement to the state's Department of Motor Vehicles, and, by obtaining a business license, you just volunteered to pay taxes to the state.

When you willingly register your transport or car within the state you reside in, you have just signed your vehicle over to the government. Now to the government, repossession is literally just that—repossession.

Also, to make the transaction official, you are then directed to place a private-prison-industry-built license plate on the car that you thought belonged to you!

THE BEAUTY OF RACISM

This is contract number two. It's called a *driver's license*, and the government has you believing that you must have one to operate a transport or car on these roads. Roads, mind you, that rest on land that doesn't belong to them, because if corporations are defined as *not real* (and they are), how can they then own *real* land?

They can't.

By this time, you have probably been issued the mark of the beast, or what is commonly known as a *social security number*. You are now told that you will need this number to work, but it's really like an account number that also doubles as some sort of tracking device.

All of us—especially men—want to provide for ourselves and our families. So you go down to your local social-security-administration building, and you start the application process.

Yet unbeknown to you, by simply jotting down what you think is an ethnicity—that is, black or African American—and signing the document, you have just solidified this fraud and set it into the full taxation and jurisdictional mode. You have essentially given the corporate state the green light to tax or steal your hard-earned money, and they also have the authority to preside over you in any matters involving court proceedings.

This is contract number three of four, and it's called the *social security card*. Out of the four contracts involved, I personally find the next one truly evil.

Why?

Because in this contract, it states any and all possessions that comes from this union will be Property of the State.

There is truly but one thing that comes from the union of man and woman, and that is the live birth of their children. For those who are married or unmarried and blindly sign this document, you have effectively signed over your children and property to the corrupt, bankrupt state.

One can clearly see now why it has become so easy for the state to take the child from the parents and/or to force *proven* unsafe vaccinations on children.

Along with your children, the other property the state claims is theirs is the home that your family resides in. If you do not pay taxes on the house you think you own, just see how long it will take for the sheriffs to come knocking and start escorting you out of your property. This can be done willingly or by force, and all of it is done at the request of another corporation—called the bank.

To the parents, a child is a blessing from The Most High, but to the corporate state, the child is property to be used for commerce or medical testing. The sooner we recognize this as a community, the better we will be.

The final contract I'm speaking of is called a *marriage license*. This is contract number four. Why would an individual need a license to get married?

This wicked scheme was invented in some corporate board-room full of European lawyers, who most likely were freemasons, and it has taken root in Babylon or Baby London, a.k.a. the United States of America.

Let us take a look at the legal definition for the word *license*: *Black's Law Dictionary* defines it "as the permission granted by competent authority to exercise a certain privilege that, without such authorization, would constitute an illegal act, a trespass, or a tort." The "competent authority" would be the now-bankrupt state or corporation pretending to be a government.

So the simple acts of getting married or operating a car are *privileges* granted by the *state* and are not a right. Yet this is only done if you have paid the required fees for a *license*; then and only then can an individual exercise his or her corporate-given privilege.

These are some very important issues that we as a community must begin to address, because in my humble opinion, this is the nucleus of European racism in America.

Why do I feel that these issues must be addressed?

Listen, we know that the system is racist, so wouldn't it make sense to know if you're contracting with a system that you and your forefathers have already deemed oppressive?

The snakes in charge of government have now managed to bring the laws of the seas—or admiralty law—onto the land. They changed the system of law without the public's knowledge. The laws of the sea require that any and everything be done in the form of a contract and signature.

And since the bankrupt republic was insolvent, they then changed the legal status of the common folk from *sovereign* to *subject*. This was done by fraud, and that's why your signature is always required when doing business with this corporation called the United States of America.

It was the US Congress who in 1845 passed an act saying that admiralty law could now come on land. This was done in secrecy to the average white citizen, so I need not explain if black people were aware of this. With the government instituting admiralty law, it basically stated that common law is no longer warranted because we—meaning you and the state—have entered into a contract.

These four applications, or contracts, which you thought were unassuming paper work needed from the state, are in reality how the European nationals enslave you and your family. It is my hope that after reading this book, you will realize that by making such assumptions, you were indeed placing you and your family in grave error.

We also know that these contracts are, in fact, provided to make one a corporate entity, or a slave, to the international banking conglomerate. Now if you don't like being identified as a European, man-made creation solely used for enriching pale-skins and their corporations, the question then becomes one of very simple and humble origins.

Who are you then?

Let us have a brief history lesson to bring a little clarity to the mysterious national origins of the so-called black people of North America. My reasons for including history in the law section of the book are quite simple.

First, I am of the belief that history and law go hand in hand. Secondly, and vastly more important is that the nationality of the so-called African in America is indeed Muur American, which directly ties black people to indigenous rights on this land. It also makes the Muurs *exempt* from all *foreign* laws. So Roman law or color of law cannot be enforced on Muurs.

To those who wish to debate this or who, for some reason, just do not believe this, I say fine.

No one can tell me what nationality has done for me or what I have witnessed it do for some of my closest friends and family. I am of the opinion that when you tell the world who you are not, you are equally responsible for telling the same world who you are.

Much of the globe knows the African American by what the European says, and that is a public relations nightmare of itself, wouldn't you agree? Since the so-called black people of North America cannot be a corporation or a creation from the mind of another human being, then in the eyes of society and the universal divine laws that govern us as a whole, again, who are you?

And on that note, there is something that has always perplexed me. Why it is that the so-called black people's history on this land-mass seems to always coincide with the arrival of the European into the Americas? Why is it that the pale-skins' version of the slave story just happens to be accepted like the gospel when the Europeans were the aggressors?

In a criminal trial of rape, we wouldn't take the word of the rapist without hearing from the victim, would we? This is exactly what is taking place when we blindly accept a story that comes from the descendants of those who committed the horrific act of slavery in the first place.

If a person or a group can kill, steal, and invade one nation of people after another, maybe—just maybe—that very nation of people would not be so forthright when it comes to telling the truth about its previous colonial "misadventures."

An African proverb states, "The story of the hunt would be much different if told by the lion." I personally find it quite humorous that black people just happen to be the direct descendants of the oldest people on the planet, and the very first human civilization on the globe, yet their existence, according to some white historians, begins around the thirteenth to the fifteenth century.

Let me begin by stating that the Muur Empire fell here in the Americas in the fifteenth century. This is no coincidence; we are the ancients of the ancients. As for the slave story, exactly what are its origins and true purpose?

For those who are unfamiliar with the slave story, I think it goes something like the European came down to "uncivilized" Africa to bring the heathens Jesus and trade some things—you know, with the locals.

Somehow they were a group of very "nice" missionary Christian folk, who came from a continent that yields very little in the form of resources, especially gold and silver. They had also just recently survived a horrible epidemic (I'm not sure exactly what it was called; I think it was the black plague.) And on top of all of that, the pale-skin nations had little to no agriculture base, because much of their continent is cold. Also, much of Europe was illiterate; this included everyone from the lowly peasant to the kings and queens.

I guess what I'm asking is, what could the European have possibly traded with? The trading part of the slave story never made much sense to me; now I know why.

According to the Europeans' version of this very effective but worn-out story, they managed to secure—according to their estimates—close to over two hundred million strong and healthy Africans. According to their version, the Europeans packed them on a few ships, ships that carried at the most four hundred people maximum and brutally transported them to the Americas...*for the very first time.*

And this took place without a war or one shot being fired. So am I to believe that the pale-skin nations just bartered with little-to-no resources with a continent with limitless natural resources?

I have often wondered what type of water-filtration system they had on board those ships, because we know that they did not drink ale and seawater for the duration of the trip. I mean, even the Europeans had to have fresh water for their survival, correct?

Since we have already covered the financial windfall that slavery was for the US economy during that time, one would think that the Europeans would have undertaken certain precautions as to ensure that their "property" was well taken care of for the four-month-long trip one way.

I say this because what the military industrial complex is to the US economy today, slavery was exactly the same for that time. Now according to the Europeans' version of the slave story, they lost upward of 70 percent of their respective cargo and still brought over 150 million people.

This is simply incredible. Who would have thought that relocating an estimated two hundred million Muurs by force or willingly from one continent to another would be so easy? Let's take into consideration the fact that it would be a logistical nightmare in this day and age and that's including today's technology and the advent of much-larger ships.

At any rate, in the eyes of the pale-skin nations, they were giving the uncivilized Africans civilization. Really? Is a thank-you in order?

All nations across the planet have, at some point in their respective histories, experienced slavery. This includes the Europeans, or Slavs, at the hands of our forefathers, the Muurs/Moors, right here in America.

The word *slave* comes from the word *Slav*! To the Europeans, the Americas was the new world, new to them but certainly not new to us, the dark-skinned, wooly-haired people of the Americas, who, as you are about to read, are the autochthonous, aboriginal people of the Americas—up to and including all of the surrounding islands.

3

History

"Know Thyself"

IT IS SAID that the above saying, *know thyself,* is written in stone in many of the pyramids that dot the globe, including here in the Americas. The pyramids in the Americas are said to be older than the ones in Ta'Muure, misnamed Egypt.

If you're thinking, "Is he, the writer, saying that there were black people (Muurs) in the Americas before the arrival of the Europeans?" Yes, that is exactly what I am saying, and it is not even up for debate.

Let us take a look at the quote from the book *Africans and Native Americans,* page 69, by author Jack Forbes:

> From 1549 through 1565 the letters of the Jesuit missionaries in Brazil usually addressed to colleagues in Portugal or Spain, frequently refers to the Americans as Negroes...In April of 1549 Manuel de Nobrega, the leader of the Jesuits, addressed a letter from Bahia to Simao Rodrigues in Lisbon in which he refers to the Portuguese

in Brazil as living in sin because of their having "many negras" and lots of children by the said "black" women. [15]

In her book *Return of the Ancient Ones*, Tiara Verdiacee Washitaw-Goston El Bey writes that

> Lewis and Clark documented everything in sight, the weather, the plants, the rocks, the minerals, the people by tribe, by habits, by color, by war-like activities and it was documented a bushy-headed tribe who did not like the red man or the white man, the black bushy-headed Washitaws. Now please explain why history did not make us aware of this important fact? It was because they went to spy on the Washitaws, a people that the good old United States had signed to be their protectorates over their rights, their land, and their property.[16]

To have a better overstanding of the above-stated quotes, we must go back a little further in history. We have been led to believe that the Native American Indian is indigenous to this land and that the white man almost killed them off, stole their land, and then procured millions of Africans from a faraway continent to become slaves.

But this quote from the author and historian Carlos Cuervo Marquez states something totally different: "It is likely that, we repeat, that long ago the 'youthful' America was also a Negro continent and that the Otomies of Mexico, the Caracols of Haiti, the Matayas of Brazil, and the Albinos of Panama are the remains of

---

15 Jack Forbes, Africans and Native Americans, Champaign, IL, University of Illinois Press, 1993, p.69

16 Tiara Verdiacee Washitaw-Goston El Bey, *Return of the Ancient Ones* (Unknown Binding, 1993), p.200

the aboriginal Negro race out of which developed later what is known as the Red or American race."[17]

The native Indian is an amalgamation of Muur/Moor and Mongolian/Chinese bloodlines. The Mongols came first as invaders and then later settled and began intermixing with the Muurs (Negroes), who were already on this land.

Also see here from the book titled the Disperse written by Nelo Dadd in it he clearly states that "the Negroes were always here, they are aborigines of the continent of the Americas and also the ancestors of the American Indian." [18]

The slave story was invented by the Vatican (Jesuits) to strip the autochthonous Muurs (blacks) of their nationality and birthright to this landmass called the Americas.

With that done, the pale-skin foreigners could now erroneously call themselves and their kind American(s), when in reality they are European nationals. When the Mongols first arrived in North America, they were met by a highly civilized, mound-building culture, whose earthen structures still stand in America to this very day.

A few of the Indigenous Muur tribes here were known as the Hopewell, and the Adena, who were the primary mound-building tribes. It is impossible for the Indians to be indigenous to this land when they, along with everyone else, share our (Muur) DNA markers. This is confirmed by the fact that there were already earthen mound-builder structures and a thriving civilization here when the Indians—Mongolian/Chinese forefathers and mothers—arrived here in North America.

---

17 C. C. Marquez, *Estudios Arqueológicos Y Ethnograficos*, vol. 1 (Madrid, Spain: Editorial-America, 1920), p.272.
18 Nelo Dadd, Disperse, Bloomington, Indiana, Xlibris Corporation, 2010, p. 130.

This also supports what many native Indians in America and the surrounding islands say when they state that they descend from the lost continent of Lemuria (Muu) and Atlantis. These ancient civilizations were once located in the Pacific and Atlantic Oceans, respectively, which casts some very serious doubt on the European-inspired, Bering Strait story.

We, as a community, must overstand the lengths and the resources the pale-skin has gone to and used in order to conceal our indigenous roots to this landmass called the America(s). It has been a secret for ages that the so-called black people (Muurs) are indigenous to the entire planet, especially the Americas.

If society were to take a common-sense approach to this trivial dilemma of finding, who were the first humans to inhabit a particular geographical area, wouldn't it make sense to determine who the aboriginal people on the planet are first?

But when dealing with race and bigotry, we see that common sense is not common at all and that things tend to get very murky. We are all well aware of the fact that the first people on the planet Earth were indeed black people, or Muurs. It is because of mental slavery that plagues a large majority of black folk that many tend to have a difficult time coming to grips with the fact that we are indeed indigenous to the Americas.

And now that we have that out the way, let us take look at one of the earliest definitions of the word *American*. Here is the 1828 *Webster's* definition of the word *American*: "a native of America originally applied to the aboriginals, or copper-colored races, found here by the Europeans, but now applied to the descendants of Europeans born in America." [19]

19 Noah Webster's American Dictionary, 1828.

Copper is a very dark skin tone that comes in many shades but never comes in pale or white. It is usually very dark brown to red or cinnamon tone. Just take a look at any old regular copper penny. It is without question that the melaninated, wooly-haired, dark-skinned people of the planet Earth commonly referred to now as Muurs are, in fact, the direct descendants of the mothers and fathers of the Human family.

The Xi People or Olmec

Who are the Xi people (pronounced *she*) commonly known as the Olmec, and what is their connection to the misnamed black people of the Americas?

The Muur Olmec are the mothers and fathers of human civilization whose origin has been speculated to be from Nuwbun, or the area known now as the Congo in East Africa, and the America(s). It was the Xi people/Olmec who formed the first dynasties of east and West Africa, Sumer, Ta'Muure/Egypt, and the Americas and all the surrounding islands.

The Olmec were also a seafaring people who prided themselves on trade, agriculture, and the arts. From the many industrious works of the Olmec came the first calendar and a game played with a stick and rubber ball, which closely resembles today's game of baseball.

The Xi people were also a deeply spiritual people, who would later settle in the Americas and start a massive empire. Its capital was in what is now called Belize. Proof of their existence in the Americas are the large, stone-head carvings made of basalt depicting Olmec warriors as well as many other artifacts that also bear witness to their presence here in the Americas pre-everybody, especially the Europeans.

It would be the Olmec who would become the founders of the once-great mystical cultures of Atlantis and Lemuria, or Muu. Many other magnificent Olmec structures were found underwater off the coast of Cuba, in what many archaeologists are calling the lost city of Atlantis.

It was the Spanish invaders who first found the large stone-head structures in 1852. Some measured eight feet in height and weighed several tons. These stones were quickly reburied because of the unmistakable Muur/African features, and some were even found with cornrow braids in their hair.

Along with the discovery of the Olmec heads came the extreme lies that the European historians said to deny the Muur/African legacy of the Olmecs. The absurd lie now—which is one I find truly amusing—is that the Olmec heads are really Indians with African features. The Europeans' excuse for the broad nose and lips on the stone heads is that the builders of the stone heads did not have the "proper tools" to thin the lips out.

Really? OK.

When the expiration date on a historically long-held lie draws near, the statements to defend said lie tend to get oh, so outrageous.

Many other Muur artifacts have also been found in North America. For example, a large majority of the buildings that house the government departments of the city of Santa Barbara in California were in indeed built by the Muurs, a fact they readily admit in their brochures.

This may be the case even with the Ta'Muure/Egyptian site named Kincaid's Caves, after the gentleman who found them, G. E. Kincaid. The site is located in the Grand Canyon.

The discovery of ancient Egyptian artifacts that were found in the Grand Canyon made the front page of the 1909 *Arizona Gazette,* but it was later discredited by the criminal organization called the Smithsonian Institute.

As of today, that entire region of the Grand Canyon where the cave was said to be found has *Egyptian* names. Also, the location where the cave exists is off-limits to all persons, even national park rangers, and it is heavily protected by armed guards from the Federal Bureau of Investigation.

Even the airspace above the disputed area is off-limits. Yet the Smithsonian and the government would have you to believe that there is nothing there and that the government's reason for all the security is your safety.

As usual, the Smithsonian Institute would deny the existence of any Egyptian artifacts in the Grand Canyon. It will even go as far to say there is no existence of any ancient Egyptian or African/ Muur artifacts in *all* the America(s)!

This, of course, is complete and utter fabrication. They say this because it is in the best interest of the European in America that you call yourselves black and that you believe you arrived in the Americas on slave ships from Africa.

They can deny this information all they want, but our presence here in the Americas is written in stone—from the large basalt stone Olmec heads to the ancient pre-Arabic Kufic script found in Nevada, which reads, "Nabi Allah Muhammad" or "Allah's prophet is Muhammad."[20]

Yes, there were ancient Muur - Muslim schools located in the southwestern part of the United States, and, yes, Al-Islam was practiced here in the Americas by Muurs. This is also verified by the several digs and rock carvings discussed in the book *Saga America* by Barry Fell.

Or maybe we should consider the Keystone and Decalogue found in Arizona, which has a picture of Moses/Musa PBUH, a

20 S.M. Imamuddin, Arabic Writing and Arab Libraries, London, Ta-Ha Publishers Ltd, p.12

pharaoh, complete with beard, turban, and throbe, which, along with the fez, is traditional Muur attire.

The Xi people/Olmec are the mothers and fathers of all nations of the earth. It is especially so here in the Americas, and that includes the Aztecs, Toltec, and Mayans as well as other Muur (Indian) nations who resided in North America, like the Cree, Washitaw, Choctaw, Yamasee, Atakapa, Karankawa, and Cherokee, plus countless others.

In fact, in 1993, the United Nations, under the Indigenous People Organization Number 21593, listed the Uaxashaktun, or Washitaw Mound-building Muurs, of America as the oldest indigenous people on the planet.

A large majority of the step pyramids, artifacts, and the famous calendar that are attributed to the Mayans by European historians were, in fact, created by the Olmec.

In order to make something, one has to exist on this plane physically. And as it relates to the Mayans, who were also Muurs, they were not here in the physical form yet and thus could not have created the pyramids or the calendar, which were all built by the Mayans forefathers—the Olmec.

According to real historical accounts, the Mayans were evicted out of the Americas by the Olmec for being blood letters and were forced to relocate to what is present-day Cambodia.

The Olmec traveled northward up from the interior of Mexico and settled in and around the Mississippi River. They would later amalgamate with the Malian Muurs from West Africa and became the Washitaw Muurs. The Washitaw Muurs would later commonly be referred to as the Mound Builders.

These mounds can still be found throughout the continental United States, along with step pyramids, the largest being in the state of Georgia. The largest earthen mound structure is found in

St. Louis, Missouri. The oldest of these mounds can be found off of the coast of Florida, on a chain of islands called Islamorada.

It is of the utmost importance for the reader to overstand that at one time *every human being on this planet* was a Muur/African for a minimum of at least one hundred fifty thousand years. That's why it is said that every twenty-six thousand years—or every new age—Muur /African history has to be retold.

I sincerely believe that this is that age or apocalypse, which by its true definition really means *to disclose or reveal knowledge*. It is now that I begin to overstand why our forefathers wrote our story in stone; it was as if they knew we would forget who we were some-day. And because of it, we would pay a horrible price.

For ones&ones who may be inquiring at this point, "Who are the Muurs?" I say that, according to *Webster's Third New International Dictionary*, the word *Muur/Moor* is defined as *all the dark-skinned* people of the globe—*especially* the Negro. The Europeans, sticking to their script, would later change this definition a few times in the years to come.

Since we now have defined the noun *Muur/Moor*, let us now de-fine the adjective *black*. According to *Merriam-Webster's Dictionary*, *black* is defined as being the darkest hue, void of light, soiled, dirty, and/or wicked or evil. *Black* also comes from the Spanish word *Negro*, which comes from the Latin word *necro*, which means *dead*. This again is describing an individual's legal status, not skin color or any other physical attributes.

Now I realize that this may rub some of you the wrong way and that you may disagree, but what we can all agree on is that the word *black* has always been associated with death. For example, let us look at the word *black* as it is defined in our society.

Do you remember the last funeral you may have attended and the color that is customarily worn to burial services? My point is that the word *black* is always associated with death or dying.

Also, our community must begin to overstand the concept of word, sound, and power. What this means is that every word carries a particular sound, which is then translated to power. This range of sounds will, in turn, give that word a particular power—negative or positive energy charge. This of course is depending on the person and his or her intent.

Just because an individual decides to identify with the adjective *black*, it doesn't change or alter the negative connotation of the word. We as a community must come to the realization that because black is an adjective, it can only *describe*. It can never *identify*.

These corporate-owned brands—like black/Negro, colored, and African American—are not nationalities. If they were, there would be a landmass associated with those names. This is the main reason why black people will never receive economic reparations from this government corporation.

To begin, let us define the word *reparations* and explain why black people will never be in receipt of them. *Merriam-Webster's Dictionary* defines the word *reparations as,* usually, compensation in money, material, labor, etc., payable to a defeated country to another country or to an individual for loss suffered during or as a result of war.

The meaning of the word *reparation* is derived from its root, *reparare* or *repair*. Now as we clearly see, per the definition, economic reparations are implemented to repair nations (countries), not chattel property (blacks and Latinos), who are unknowingly bound to the corporate state via fraudulent contracts.

If the so-called black men and women are classified as chattel property by way of fraudulent contracts—and they are—why would *this* government ever consider repairing *you?*

Reparations are used to repair nations, placing victims back into the state they were in before the war. Now according to this definition, this reparation process, as it relates to black people, should most certainly involve assistance in returning to nationhood.

The issue is that, as it relates to African Americans, or blacks, they are asking for said reparations from the position of a slave—a slave who also happens to think he or she has no nation or nationality to return to. This thought process flourishes because a majority of our community believes that the slave trade happened without a war or one shot being fired.

Yet while all of this transpires, the US government pretends like it doesn't know who you truly are, and it does so because it is looking out for its best interest—the corporate interest. This scheme is required in order keep this racial color game in perpetual existence.

The chattel brands *black* and *white* are, in reality, nothing more than legal statuses that denote a form of a hidden caste system in America. It is a caste system which, much like India's, routinely finds the so-called black people last in every societal category.

A very dear friend of mine once stated, "Black people need to do their own public-relations campaign."

"Why do you feel like that?" I asked him.

He answered, "Because we, as a community, always allow white people to tell *our* story!"

Please listen very closely. It is impossible for a European national— or anyone else, for that matter—to tell our story. That is akin to your four-year-old son attempting to tell his grandmother her history and the place she originated from. It's just not possible, and it is also very disrespectful to do so.

This is only made possible when you have much of the black community being afflicted with the condition called *slave mentality*. All people with Muur ancestry have it, but there is one difference between you and me: I recognize that I have the condition called *slave mentality*, and since I recognize it, I can address it.

Now we have had a brief history lesson about our glorious ancestors called the Xi people. Please note that I have attempted to be brief. One would have to dedicate an entire series of books to the Olmec, and that still would not be enough.

The nationality and birthright of the so-called black people in America is Muur descent, and they should be properly titled Muur American. This nationality directly links you with your ancestors the Olmec, who were also of Muur descent.

It was our ancestors, the Muurs, who gave specific European nations the right to start thirteen colonies and to do commerce in our homeland called Al Muroc/Al Maghrib Al Aska, or Turtle Island, later named America.

Proof of this existing deal is the Star Spangled Banner, which symbolizes European commerce on Muur lands. That banner is currently mistaken for the flag of the US government.

Simply throw out everything you have learned about history, as it relates to black people in the America(s).

It was the Avatar who, in truth, stated, "Nationality is the order of the day." If that is so—and it is—then the more important question becomes, what is your nationality? Nationality comes from the word *natural*, which, in turn, comes from the word *nature*, which means land.

The unconscious Moors of America, who are now referred to as African Americans, have been criminally denationalized by deceitful contracts and this was done for the sole purpose of placing you under the jurisdiction of the foreign European powers. The pale-skins are essentially enforcing Roman or European law commonly known as *civil law*, thousands of miles away from Rome or Europe and on Muur lands.

All of this happens as the so-called African American collective is busy slumbering and bickering over issues that absolutely play no role in removing this dark cloud I refer to as racism. And because of these trivial diversions, our community is paying a very heavy price for it.

Muur science, or Sufi Islam, teaches that the five components that make a natural person are as follows:

1. Body
2. Soul
3. Spirit
4. Nationality
5. Religious creed

Now out of the five that are listed, only two can be given or taken away, and they would be *nationality* and *creed*. So according to our ancestral teachings, *creed* is defined as the path of God's consciousness established through your foremothers and forefathers' vine and fig tree. Or, simply put, how your ancestors worshipped God.

It is part of our oral history that the five civilized Muur tribes were called civilized by the invading European powers because the tribal leaders readily accepted Christianity. It is also to be noted that the leaders of the tribes accepted Christianity, but it still took a long process for the people of the tribes to accept the European version of the religion.

Now back to the sciences.

The number five in the science of numerology symbolizes completeness. This takes us to the three-fifths slave-tax clause that was written into the US Constitution.

Once *nationality* and *creed* were either given up and/or brutally beaten out of the recently defeated Muurs, it paved the way for the European colonial powers to introduce Christianity to the newly enslaved Moors. The pale-skin freemasons, who were and are still in government, also received their teaching from our Muur forefathers.

The freemasons knew of the concept of five components that makes up a natural human being, and the Muurs, while being stripped of nationality and creed, were now considered subhuman because of said loss. This was done after the ruling European masonic powers had twisted our sciences, broken treaties, made war, and then denationalized the Muurs.

They then forced Christianity onto the Muurs. These two acts (Christianity and the stripping of nationality) alone have paved the way for the continued enslavement of so-called black people in America. From the past, right up until this present day, nothing has really changed at all.

We have also learned from the three-fifths slave-tax clause that it had nothing to do with taxes and everything to do with the continuous concealment of the so-called black people's national origin. Couple that with us knowing the lowly rank of a slave in any given society, how can anyone or anybody tax a slave, who in the eyes of many a European were now considered below human form?

This deception has reaped huge financial benefits for the foreign European nations, while the exact deception has led to the spiritual and economic destruction of large portions of the so-called black community. The ginormous advantage the pale-skins have over the unconscious Muurs is that they know that you so-called blacks are Muurs by birthright and nationality. They also know that this is Muur land, which, in turn, makes it *your* land.

Our problem is we do not know who we are. Yet what is even more troubling is that many black people don't even care to know. And for those who know, a large majority of them have taken secret oaths to continue hiding what is being revealed in this book. It was Noble Drew Ali who said, "In the coming months and years even the Prince Hall Mason will have to bear witness to his true national name."

4

Religion or Christianity

Knowledge makes a man unfit to be a slave.

—FREDERICK DOUGLASS

IT APPEARS THAT in the case of a large majority of black people and the American public in general, many have been conditioned by society—or the ruling minority—to think that discussing religion and politics is somehow a taboo, an off-limits subject.

Well, not me. I'm also in total disagreement with this ridiculous notion. As a matter of fact, I personally enjoy discussing these so-called hot-button issues—except for politics—because currently I have no use for politics.

So for now, we will focus our attention on religion and the effects European Christianity has had and continues to have over our community. The European in America attempts to control the narrative as it relates to religion or slavery by simply not addressing these matters, especially as they pertain to black people in America.

That's because the topics of racism and slavery will and should come up. The reason I feel that it doesn't come up is because the Europeans in America simply do not want their number-one control mechanism to be exposed, and that is *Christianity.*

It was Noble Drew Ali who coined the term *slave mentality. Slave mentality* is a mental illness that afflicts the minds of so-called black people in America. It is a by-product of slavery, denationalization, Jim Crow laws, and this system of racial injustice.

If the condition called slave mentality is a sickness, then the religion of Christianity is the virus that brought it on. Even the pale-skins will admit that they violently imposed their faith on the newly defeated slaves as solely a matter of *controlling* them.

All you have to do is to drive through any urban or ghetto area and you will witness social decay that is masked by the ever-increasing installation of small churches and megachurches into the area. How can a multimillion-dollar megachurch be justifiably built in some of the poorest neighborhoods in this country?

When you see that the rationale behind building these structures is about control and not feeding the human spirit, then and only then can you fully overstand this spiritual predicament.

The psychological effects of worshipping your known oppressor's God may never be truly overstood. We do know that there are some real effects the religion of Christianity has had on the hearts and minds of black folk, and that spell continues to this very day.

The Europeans knew that they were dealing with a very spiritual people, so they made promises of paradise that was the dream that was often sold to the slaves. The Christian heaven that the Europeans spoke of could only be obtained through obedience and hard work in the fields, according to the ruling, foreign powers.

It would be those very same Europeans who as plantation owners who would brutally separate the slaves who still spoke their native language from those who didn't. This was all done in an effort
to get the slave to transition more quickly to Christianity. Control
of product is vital, I suppose.

Also the ruling Christians would violently separate slaves
from their families because the pale-skins knew that worship
had been a family and communal practice by the Muurs. When
the family was destroyed, it also destroyed many cultural and
spiritual practices as well.

But before we delve into the European version of Christianity,
it is very important for the reader to overstand that all major reli-
gions have their roots in Ethiopia/Ta'Muure (land of the Muurs)
and the America(s).

Let us begin.

We can trace the European's form of Christianity back to 325ad
in what was called the Council of Nicaea, which convened to address the divinity of the one called Jesus Christ. This gathering
also included all Christian bishops from around Europe and the
emperor of Rome at that time, Emperor Constantine.

The sole purpose of this conference was to raise Jesus PBUH,
a man born of a woman, to the status of God. Then they had to
reconstruct the Bible to fit this narrative and implement what today is called the Holy Trinity—which is the Vatican's religious doctrine. This doctrine defines the father God, the son Jesus Christ,
and the Holy Spirit as one entity.

It was now stated as religious fact...well, at least according to
the attendees of the conference. And as a matter of solidifying this
decree, anyone who disagreed with this new edict was considered
a heathen or an unbeliever and would most certainly be enslaved
and/or put to death.

During this time, all Europeans were considered Christian, because people of color *were*, of course, "people of color." This fact alone disqualified Muurs/Africans from being Christians, thus making us heathens or nonbelievers in the eyes of the Christian European powers.

It would be the Roman Catholic Church, the head of European Christianity, that would purposely mistranslate and misuse certain verses in the Bible to sanction the brutal practice of slavery over the defeated Muurs of the Americas and abroad. The lasting effects of this tragedy are still pulsating through our community today.

It is one thing to love God or any God for that matter. But it is an entirely different subject when you love the God of your known subjugator. Because loving the God of your oppressor means that eventually those of you who are being oppressed will begin to no longer view your oppressor as the aggressor.

When that happens, you will have a generation of people who have now become spoiled with bondage, and this is exactly where the African American community is at this very moment.

What has the God of European Christianity actually taught the pale-skin nations? It is their actions alone that would leave one to think that those teachings included the horrific practices of slavery, land stealing, and denationalization of a people. The intentional raping and killing of women and children served the desired plot of destroying the Muur family structure.

I was taught years ago that Satan has many names and that one of those names he calls himself is god. One has to think, just what God were the Europeans worshipping while committing these atrocities?

As a side note, the root word for *Christian* is *cretin*, which means idiot, half-wit, imbecile, or village retard.

"The story of the hunt will be quite different if the lion tells his side of the story." (Old Moorish proverb)

To be very clear, slavery did exist; it just did not take place as the Europeans said it did. The slave story was created and embellished as a way to explain how millions of Moors/Africans ended up on the shores of the Americas. The story was basically grafted to mask our indigenous presence in the Americas, particularly North America.

The pale-skin nations did not bring Muurs/Africans to the Americas for the very first time; the pale-skin nations enslaved the Muurs who were already here. Then they started kidnapping Muurs from the Americas to Europe and then to Africa and then later they kidnapped Muurs from Africa and shipped them to the Americas and Europe.

The invading European forces overstood that they were dealing with a divine people—the fallen Muurs. They also recognized that by replacing the religious creed of Al-Islam as well as other indigenous beliefs with Christianity, they would subdue and essentially control the defeated Muurs for hundreds of years to come.

This cruel tactic has most certainly been effective.

To begin this journey, let us start by taking a look at the following Bible verses that the European Christians used to validate slavery. Let us start with the Old Testament. Leviticus 25:44–45 states, "Your male and female slaves are to come from the nations around you; from them you may buy slaves. You may also buy some of the temporary residents living among you and members of their clan born in your country, and they will become your property."

Or let's take a look this one. According to Ephesians 6:5–6, "Slaves, obey your earthly masters with fear and trembling, in singleness of heart, as you obey Christ; not only while being watched, and in order to please them, but as slaves of Christ, doing the will of God from the heart."

OK. Let us take a look at this one. The verse 1 Peter 2:13 commands, "Submit yourselves for the Lord's sake to every authority instituted among men." This is one of many from the New Testament. It is a historical fact that the New Testament was not in existence when Jesus (PBUH) walked the earth, and it was the early church fathers that would sanction slavery.

The Catholic priest St. Thomas Aquinas said, "Slavery among men is natural, for some are naturally slaves." The vicious act of enslaving another human being for any reason was embedded in the highest sections of the papacy. Here's a quote from Pope Nicholas V:

> Well therefore weighing all and singular the premises with due meditation, and noting that since we had formerly by other letters of ours granted among other things free and ample faculty to the aforesaid King Alfonson— to invade, search out, capture, vanquish, and subdue all Saracens [Moors] and pagans whatsoever, and other enemies of Christ where so ever placed, and the kingdoms, dukedoms, principalities, dominions, possessions, and all moveable and immovable goods whatsoever held and possessed by them and to reduce their persons to perpetual slavery.[21]

The words *Saracen*, *Muur*, and *African* were used interchangeably to describe the darker-skinned people of the planet during that time. In an unbridled display of arrogance, the Roman Catholic Church openly admits to altering and changing the Bible as well as endorsing the violent conquest of the Muurs.

---

21 Thomas Aquinas, *Summa Theologica* (New York Benziger Bros, 1947).

Finally here's a law passed by the newly formed pale-skin colonies in the state of Virginia in 1670. Here the reader will clearly see that the Roman Catholic Church and the colonial government were, and still are, in perfect harmony when it came to the continued physical and economic enslavement of the Muurs here and abroad. The law, the Virginia Slave Act, states, "All servants not being Christian, imported into this colony by shipping, shall be slaves for their lives."

It was this type of mind-set that eventually morphed itself into what the Europeans would later dub *manifest destiny*. This practice was widely accepted by the pale-skin nations who believed that they had been blessed to conquer the Americas and the surrounding islands.

We know that things can indeed get lost in translation. Only this appears to be a systemic decision on the part of the European powers to not only enslave those whom they felt were unbelievers to their newfound faith called Christianity but also enslave them forever.

True history and linguistics have proved that the original language of the first Bible was in Geez, which is the father of all Ethiopian Semitic languages including Aramaic, Hebrew, and Arabic, which *all* happen to be Moor/African dialects. Much of the early biblical manuscripts are, in fact, actual copies of ancient Ta'Muure script. This may also explain why the first Ta'Muure (Egyptian) dynasties said that their religious creeds or gods came from the south, meaning Ethiopia.

The Bible is, without a doubt, an African story, which takes place in that region (and the Americas as well), and it is also a book of historical reference for the forgotten Muurs of America. Yet before today's holy Bible is even opened for the reader, he or she should immediately take notice of the words *version* written on the front of the book.

This is critical, so let us define the word *version*: a particular form of something differing in certain respects from an earlier form or other forms of the same type of thing.

The Council of Nicaea and the Roman Catholic Church still have a very difficult time explaining Jesus's (PBUH) Catholic God status, when even he had a beginning and an end. The Bible says that his beginnings started in David's loins, according to Acts 2:29–30, and he violently ended on the cross, according to the Roman Catholic Church.

Also according to the European Christians, the Muurs were cursed through the biblical figure Ham. Because of this curse, the Christians are now justified to make war with the Muurs, enslave them, and take their land.

How convenient.

Let's take a closer look at this alleged curse. It first appears as a European Jewish story with roots in the Talmud. Secondly, according to the Bible, the curse was on Canaan and not Ham.

The ruling pale-skin nations would also have you believe that Ham is the father of *all* the African nations, which is impossible, considering that we Muurs have inhabited this landmass called Earth for millions of years—before the Bible and/or any other holy text existed. I am personally of the belief that no one truly knows our origins, only the creator, because as Muur/African people, we are old as creation itself.

The Bible is a Muur/African history book that has been tampered with, yet it is still full of truth and describes a lot of the conditions we find ourselves in today.

Now let us get back to this curse.

When you study the curse of Ham, you will see that it was not Ham but Canaan that was cursed with leprosy. According to 2 Kings 5:27, "The leprosy therefore of Naaman shall cleave unto thee, and unto thy seed forever. And he went out from his presence a leper as white as snow."

Leprosy is a disease that turns the skin white and makes one's hair grow blond and straight out of his or her scalp, not curly or in spirals like 9Ether hair, misnamed *nappy* hair. We Muurs, the melaninated, wooly-haired people of the globe, do not and have never possessed white skin and blond hair growing straight out of our scalp. This appears to be a European affliction.

Please overstand and note that the religion of Christianity is not bad or wrong at all. It is just happens to be bad and wrong for the indigenous peoples of the Americas who are Muurs by birthright and nationality.

These unconscious Muurs, who have now been denationalized and branded *black* or *African American*, have the right to worship under their own vine and fig tree, like every other person on this planet. If only the European powers would have honored and respected such a wise sentiment, Moors could have avoided a lot of pain and suffering.

Now on a final note, there may be some of you who are aware of the historical role the Ashkenazi (European) Jew and the amalgamated Arabs played in the slave trade. Let us start with the money changers. We will address the Jewish role for starters.

According to Rabbi Marc Lee Raphael, "Jews also took an active part in the Dutch colonial slave trade; indeed, the bylaws of the Recife and Mauricia congregations [1648] included an imposta (Jewish tax) of five soldos for each Negro slave a Brazilian Jew purchased from the West Indies Company. Slave auctions were postponed if they fell on a Jewish Holiday"[22]

22 Rabbi Marc L. Raphael, Jews and Judaism in the United States: A Documentary History, New York, Behrman House, 1983, p. 14 23-25.

As I mentioned earlier in this chapter, it was in the Eastern European Jew's religious text called the Talmud where the origins of the so-called curse of Ham can be found. We can clearly see that the Bible and the Talmud have been used to justify the enslavement of the Muurs here in America.

Before we address the Arabs and Islam, I must state that as a Muslim myself, I may admittedly be a little biased, of course, when covering this topic, but I will do my best to be fair.

I have often heard the statement that the Arabs used the religion of Al Islam to enslave the Muurs. First, let us establish few things about Islam and its relationship with the Muurs.

For starters, the very language of Islam and that the Holy Quran it is written in is called Arabic, an African or Muur dialect. That means that before the amalgamated Arab came into existence, Africans or Muurs were already speaking the language and practicing Islam.

Also, the beautiful sound of the call to prayer, or the Adhan, was first instituted by an ex-slave by the name of Bilal PBUH. Bilal was freed from bondage by the Prophet Muhammad PBUH.

The original Arabians were Muurs. It is no accident or coincidence that the oldest version of the Holy Quran is in the hands of the Muurs of West Africa. And according to the Holy Quran, the religion of Al Islam is the religion of Ibrahim or Abraham El, not An-Nabi Muhammad Mustapha El-Amin or the Prophet Muhammad, peace be unto both prophets, who were both Muurs.

Let us now take a look at the following verse from the Holy Quran. In 3:95, it says, "Allah speaketh the truth: follow the religion of Abraham, the sane in Faith; he was not of the Pagans." For those of you who are asking, "Just who was Abraham or Ibrahim El PBUH?" I have this answer: the Holy Prophet Ibrahim El was a Muur from the City of Ur in Chaldea, present-day Basra, Iraq.

In the book *From Babylon to Timbuktu*, Professor Rudolph Windsor states "that Abraham's father was from the land of Ur of the Chaldees, Genesis 11:26-28. The Chaldeans were one of the Cushite tribes. Cush means black, according to the Bible dictionary."[23] See also Godfrey Higgins, a renowned English antiquarian, who states, "The Chaldeans were originally Negroes."[24]

It has been reported that when the invading forces of the US military entered the city of Basra, Iraq, they were stunned to find that the original inhabitants of the city looked just like the so-called black people of America.

This is interesting because the Prophet Abraham, or Ibrahim El PBUH, is the forefather of the Children of Israel, or the Muurs. He was such an upright man that Allah swt considers him a friend— something that I personally find amazing.

Now let us take a look at what the Holy Quran says about the Arabs and the practice of slavery. We will begin with the Arab people. In 9:97, it states, "The Arabs of the desert are the worst in unbelief and hypocrisy, and most fitted to be in ignorance of the command which Allah hath sent down to his Messenger but Allah is All-Knowing, All Wise."

And in 9:101, we find, "Certain of the desert Arabs round about you are Hypocrites, as well as (desert Arabs) among The Madinah folk: they are obstinate in hypocrisy: thou knowest them not: We know them: twice shall We punish them: and in addition shall they be sent to a grievous punishment."

Do ones&ones still believe that the Arabs gave the Muurs the religion of Al Islam and used said religion to enslave the Muurs? I hope you do not. At least you shouldn't.

---

23 Rudolph R. Windsor, From Babylon to Timbuktu, Ancient Black Civilization, New York, Windsor Golden Series, 2003, p.16

24 Godfrey Higgins, Anacalypsis, Vol. II, New York, Digireads.com, 1927, p. 364

Let us continue and see what the book says about the evil and cruel practice of slavery. In 90:11–16, the Holy Quran says, "But he attempts not the uphill road; and what will make thee comprehend what the uphill road is? (It is) to free a slave, or to feed in a day of hunger an orphan nearly related. Or the poor man lying in the dust."

We can now bear witness that, yes, the European, Christian powers did, in fact, use certain verses in the Bible to justify the enslavement of the Muurs globally. And that justification was derived from a so-called curse, which had its roots in the European, Jewish Talmud. We are also well aware of the role the desert Arabs played in the Muur/African slave trade.

But it is the humble opinion of this writer that, according to the verses I quoted, slavery was not sanctioned in the Islamic text as a justification for the oppression of the defeated Muurs/Moors—or for anyone, for that matter. Also, let us be very clear: The Arabs are not the founders of the religion of Al Islam. Last but not least, certain Arabs are not mentioned in a very good light in these verses quoted from the Holy Quran.

It appears that the European Jew, the Christians, and the Arabs did whatever was necessary to culturally bury the recently defeated Muurs. Thus by doing so, in the process, they increased their economic wealth via the brutal slave trade. These three parties intended to achieve their desired goals by any means necessary, even if that meant lying and distorting holy texts.

So be it.

Now, the willful mistranslation of holy text is not an issue of concern for the amalgamated Arab, because unlike the European Jew or Christian, the Arabs speak and write Arabic, which again is a Muur/African dialect.

The Arab also believes but does not necessarily follow certain tenets of Al Islam. I say this because certain Arabs willfully enslave and kill their fellow Muslim believers and treat them in a manner that is less than human or is unfitting even for them.

We also know that individuals from within our very own community have also benefited greatly from the slave-trade story. This is because the cruel practice of enslaving the many for the well-being of the few is still very much a common occurrence even in this day and age.

5

Entertainment

To some people, employment is a distraction.
To all entertainers, distraction is employment.

—MOKOKOMA MOKHONOANA

IT IS OF no accident or coincidence that the warmongering US government—you know, the one that leads the nations of the world in bombs dropped on humans—is also the leader in the world of entertaining those humans.

That's at least while they are still among the living.

Being the world's leader in military destructive capabilities while at the same time holding the badge as the entertainment capital of the world is all part of the grand plan.

Some may argue—including me—that the two most effective weapons in the arsenal of the ruling European powers are the unconscious soldier and the well-paid but misinformed entertainer.

I am of the personal belief that the corporate-owned media might be more dangerous than the military fighter jet. As we dig deeper into this chapter, it will become very apparent the true purpose of this phenomenon called *entertainment.*

This phenomenon, entertainment, and its close cousin, television, both play the role of the conduit, meaning that they ensure that the government's lies get funneled directly to the ears of the public, thus guaranteeing that the distraction goes on. This may explain why our society is practically brainwashed by way of television programming. No other citizenry on the planet watches more television than the population of the United States of America.

My father, mentor, and teacher, the Honorable Jah Prophet Hobsoni, stated, "The entertainment industry tells lies using vision." Get it -*Tell-lie-vision*, which is a very accurate depiction indeed.

Let's take a look at the definition of *entertainment* and see if it is applicable to our situation in this country. *Entertainment* is defined as the act of entertaining—agreeable *occupation* for the mind, *diversion*, and amusement. It comes from the Greek and breaks down the following way:

- enter: come into
- tain: possess or hold
- ment: state of being

As we see, per the definition, entertainment can be used for mere amusement, or it can be used as a *diversion* or both. What is it that this society needs diverting from, one may ask.

Here is a perfect example of just that.

It has been widely reported that the Monica Lewinsky sex scandal involving former president Bill Clinton was just a diversion to mask the illegal bombing of the sovereign country of Yugoslavia.

If that tactic was successful—and it was—you can be assured that it has been repeated.

We are all familiar with the timeless adage *if it ain't broke, don't fix it*. Well, it most definitely applies here.

Another glaring example of this is the following quote from David Rockefeller, founder of the Trilateral Commission. In an address to a meeting of The Trilateral Commission in June 1991, he stated,

> We are grateful to the *Washington Post*, the *New York Times*, *Times Magazine*, and other great publications whose directors have attended our meetings and respected their promises of discretion for almost forty years. It would have been impossible for us to develop our plan for the world if we had been subject to the bright lights of publicity during those years. But, the work is now much more sophisticated and prepared to march toward a world government. The supranational sovereignty of an intellectual elite and world bankers is surely preferable to the national auto determination practiced in past centuries. [25]

As I stated in the previous chapter, the Rockefeller family are part owners of the privately owned Federal Reserve banking system. This is one of the main reasons why the American trend forecaster Gerald Celente coined the term *presstitute* as it relates to the US media.

He used the term to describe US media because the so-called press in America is just a sad combination of prostitutes and press and is nothing more than a highly paid government mouthpiece for endless propaganda and entertainment masking itself as real news.

---

25 Gyeorgos C. Hatonn, Programming, Pitfalls and Puppy-Dog Tales, Phoenix Source, 1993, p.65

Besides the sex scandal, we also have to thank the Clinton Administration for the corporate consolidation of American media. It was under his watch that nearly all media—newspaper, magazines, television, news stations, radio, and book-publishing companies—were consolidated by private corporations.

According to Vic Bishop, in the article "The Illusion of Choice: Ninety Percent of American Media Is Controlled by Six Corporations," the following mega corporations—Comcast, News Corp, Disney, Viacom, Time Warner, and CBS—control 90 percent of what the American public read, watch, and listen to.

In the article, Mr. Bishop also says, "Those numbers average out to one media executive controlling what 850,000 people see, read, and hear as it pertains to news and or entertainment in this country."[26]

These are mind-blowing numbers. Now is it any wonder why all news and entertainment is basically repeating itself as an endless cycle of worthless news? This usually is followed up with a ridiculous story about some celebrity, which has no real bearing on issues that affect your life or the lives of your family members for that matter.

Remember, entertainment is defined as a *diversion*.

The powers that be obviously want to control what the American public and much of the world considers newsworthy. They also use entertainment as a convenient distraction when and where they deem necessary.

Those who are in control of media and entertainment have an enormous advantage. First, they can tell any- and everyone's story and beam it around the globe. This is done regardless of the truth and accuracy of the said story or plot.

---

26 Vic Bishop, The Illusion of Choice: Ninety Percent of American Media Is Controlled by Six Corporations, Globalreseacrh.ca, August 29th 2015, p. 1-4.

The European media generally paint all black people and people of color in a bad light, while they are always vigilant about how their white image is being portrayed. As we have constantly seen, white people (men in particular) are often portrayed as the hero, at least in their minds and in the movies.

It was my empress who pointed out this difference as it relates to TV news stations and the way that they report local crimes. She demonstrated masterfully that she knows when a black person allegedly commits a crime because the news stations will come outright and say that a black person did it.

The flipside of course is when a white person or even a Latino allegedly commits a crime the ethnic makeup of them isn't always made known, but every time a black person allegedly commits a crime, his or her racial background is immediately aired and shown. In this respect, the media are always consistent and remain true to form.

Is it any surprise that the Europeans in America incessantly show themselves and their community in a more than favorable image than anyone else? How many Hollywood movies have we seen where the white actor plays the role of a Muur, Chinese, Indian, and anyone else the makeup artist could make up!

And do we have to endure another movie about the totally bogus claims of Europeans being indigenous to Northeast Amexxum or North Africa, particularly Ta'Muure, commonly misnamed Egypt? How is that possible when according to European scientists and historians, the pale-skin race is just a little over sixty-five hundred years old, as reported by the prestigious National Geographic Society?

Professor Alan Cooper, the director of the Australian Centre for Ancient DNA at the University of Adelaide, confirmed this when he analyzed DNA from ancient skeletons and found that the genetic makeup of the modern European was established just sixty-five hundred years ago.

Professor Cooper's findings are very interesting and yet confusing, because no one truly knows how old the pyramids are in Ta'Muure/Egypt and also because real history and archaeology have confirmed that the pyramids and earthen mound structures found here in the Americas may be just as old as, or even older than, those found in North Africa.

There are many problems with the "Europeans built the structures in Egypt" theory. But one very simple fact is that the Europeans, according to their own scientists, were not in creation as of yet. And no one truly knows how old the pyramids in Ancient Egypt are, but we do know they are far older than sixty-five hundred years old.

Even now, as our Muur presence is being discovered in the America(s) pre-everybody, there are some within the European community who feel that the mounds and pyramids found in the America(s) were built by white people.

Again, this is delusional and a sad state of denial, because the earthen mound structures and pyramids were built by the Washitaw mound-builder Muurs, in particular, the Adena and Hopewell tribes, who are still located to this day in West Virginia.

This blatant lie is only made possible because European nationals own and operate much of today's print media and entertainment corporations. That means that they can write themselves into ancient history via movies and blogs, all while *not* being an ancient people.

The reverse of this, of course, is the feeble attempt to write out black people—a very old people, mind you—from ancient history, or any other history for that matter. This is only accomplished by the Europeans' global monopoly on the mass media. I say again, the media are the Europeans' most deadly weapon.

As we have witnessed in the past, before the actual bombs are dropped on the so-called enemy, the enemy is first dehumanized by the media. It is usually done under the direction of the CIA or some other military consultant.

This takes place because the government has mastered the art of brutalizing and discrediting its perceived adversary. It is this tactic that makes it very easy for the soldier to kill what he now perceives as a threat to him and his way of life.

The media will always use words like *evil, despot,* or *thug* to describe any one individual, community, or state that they feel is getting out of line. Indeed our very own people have adopted this way of thinking and acting.

See, when a black man views his fellow man as just a dog or a nigga, it then becomes very easy to kill or bring harm to him, because neither of those words is used to properly describe a man or human being. So if for some reason the man feels that he must harm him, in his mind, he is not hurting a fellow brother/Muur or human.

No, he's just a dog or nigga, and these derogatory labels have been purposely imbedded into the subconscious via television programming.

The same can then be said about the vile act of prostituting a woman, or Wombman, for a man's monetary gain. Again, it is very easy to put a bitch or a hoe out on the stroll to get that 'chedda' for you, but it is impossible to put an Empress out there.

Another example of this is a young black man growing up in Los Angeles, California. Black people, especially the youth, were often told by the corporate media that we should not expect to live past the age of twenty-five. This, of course, was repeatedly done over and over again in some sort of attempt at brainwashing us.

When, as a youth, you are constantly being bombarded by the media that you should not expect to live past such a young age, you may begin to feel that you must experience it all now; even if that means that some of you may endure some horrific consequences along the way.

Now add drugs and gang influence into the mind of that young person, and it becomes very clear why our neighborhoods have become breeding grounds for young men and women who truly do not care about their lives as well as the lives of others.

A large majority of the US population is well aware of the overt sexism and violence portrayed in today's media. Sex and violence are used to sell any and everything under the sun, and it is done so blatantly that they have even coined a term for the practice. It is simply called *sex sells*.

The media have an agenda, and that agenda appears to be the dumbing down of the masses by any means necessary. This is underway while the media also make it appear that certain acts like homosexuality and the unnecessary usage of violence to solve some of the most trivial of problems are the norm and essentially OK.

European media in America have a new pet project now. They now want to incite a race war between blacks and whites, with hopes of bringing about civil unrest. The evil ones in charge will try this while preparing for phase two of their plan, which is the illegal attempt at gun confiscation and martial law, all of which will lead to more violence, and this, by the way, is again the desired plan.

We have seen part of this plan play out with the current president of the United States, Donald Trump, whose rallies, when campaigning for office, resembled nothing more than updated Klu Klux Klan (KKK) meetings, only this time it played out in front of the world. Once again, it was the old divide and conquer method tried countless times in history, which proves it has been vastly successful.

There are two words that can sum up American media: *consumerism* and *entertainment.* When a person is consumed with consumption, he or she does so at the risk of his or her attention being diverted from the more serious things that truly pose a threat to the earth and her earthlings.

The following quote from the Holy Quran appears quite troubling for many black people and people in general because while most are fixated on the consumption of material goods, their attention is constantly being diverted by the daily dose of news, entertainment, and racism, which is, of course, all planned.

As it says in the Holy Quran 102:1, "The mutual rivalry for piling up (the good things of this world) diverts you (from the more serious things)."

When the diversion is accomplished, our community may miss the opportunity to reclaim our nationality and overstand the importance of nation building and self-governance.

To put it simply, while we are busy being thoroughly entertained and entertaining, our attention has been funneled away from matters of grave importance—like addressing our political status—that will greatly assist us in our fight against global white supremacy.

To ensure that blacks remain in this trancelike state, the pale-skin nations have employed an array of some of the most powerful and sinister organizations to do just that. Some operate out in the open. Others do not, but how they operate is irrelevant when the stated agenda is the same.

One of the first and foremost of these organizations that come to mind is the masonic-inspired Black Boulé. It is one of the oldest African American Greek secret societies. It was founded in 1904 by Dr. Henry Minton and five of his colleagues.

The Black Boulé's stated mission was to recruit professional blacks into its ranks, and those blacks would then shape the thought process of the average black person. It was also the stated objective of the Boulé to keep the so-called black professional away from the growing Marcus Garvey movement, which was a back-to-Africa philosophy stressing self-awareness and community empowerment.

The unification of the Marcus Garvey movement with the black professionals would have greatly benefited the black community. But it would *not* have been of any assistance to the ruling white society.

While being a masonic society, the Boulé operates much like a pyramid scheme, meaning that the lower ranks are not aware of the grand plan that the higher ranks are privy to. It also has been reported that every black leader and well-known entertainer is a part of this treasonous network.

Although these networks of so-called black-elite celebrities operate in secret, they are clearly supported by the white ruling elite. So, let me be very clear: The Boulé does not serve the interest of the black community. No, it is a self-serving society that gets its orders and sustenance from the ruling European elite, commonly referred to as the Illuminati.

As Steve Cokely said, "Anywhere there are prominent Blacks; chances are they're in the Boulé."

The blue and white colors of the Boulé are symbolic of service to a Greek king, not service to the black community, according to several Greek definitions.

The Boulé's influence is deep rooted and intense, and they are well financed. For the European elite to maintain their power and influence over the Boulé, much has been reported about the homosexual acts that the ultra-secretive group indulges in and that these acts are used as some type of initiation process to gain entry into this group.

My guess is—and it may be safe to say—that if people choose to indulge in such practices, the acts could very well be recorded and archived for future blackmail purposes. I believe that this is done just in case a Boulé member suddenly gets a conscience and starts to look out for self and his community. The European elite will then use that information to blackmail the individual into getting back in the evil ones' program, or that person can be just outright terminated.

Proof of this plot, some will say, is the turn hip-hop has undertaken the last decade or so. The over glorification of the gangsta mentality is now somehow coupled with a deliberate march toward sanctioning homosexuality as an OK sexual act.

This homosexual agenda is being force fed to my community with the aid of music and television. Until this point, rap music has generally been about obtaining capital wealth and materialism—nothing new in rap. But it is this new way of thinking that has had devastating effects on our community in more ways than one can imagine.

We know this mind-set of "get rich or die trying" serves to only to strengthen white corporations, particularly the private-prison industry. This is usually the end game for the many who want to obtain said capital and material goods at any cost and fail.

They have a place for those individuals as well, and it is called the US justice system. The Department of Justice operates in conjunction with the privately owned, white prison system, and they both benefit economically from the warehousing of black people.

Additionally, we now have the private-prison companies, which are suing the states where their prisons are located because the state did not meet their desired prisoner quotas. You see, these prison companies get paid per inmate and bed, so it is very lucrative for them to keep the beds filled.

Also, the prison industry is the only obstacle that is preventing the decriminalization of the herb that is misnamed marijuana. This will also explain why blacks and Latinos are warehoused in jails for nonviolent drug offenses that usually involve the herb.

The "fuck it get paid" mentality that many in rap have adopted may have direct implications for the ever-increasing profit margin shared by the pale-skin who chooses to invest in America's private-prison system. And while the institution of slavery was big business back then, the private-prison complex is the equivalent of it today.

I simply call it *slavery 2.0.*

The current status of the rap game is all about getting money at any cost while disrespecting anyone in the process, especially the black woman. This is very troubling considering that a nation is judged by how it treats its women, elderly, and children.

As I stated previously in this chapter, in American society *sex sells.* And since we all know that sex has always existed in the music and hip-hop industry, this homosexual agenda that is now taking place in the rap game today is an entirely different topic.

I mean a few male rappers and actors have actually begun to wear dresses!

One has to be either blind and/or dead not to see the obvious homosexual scheme being played out in music, film, and television. This scheme appears to be directed at the black community and shows like *Empire* are proof of this televised plot.

The creators of these shows and others like them are merely part of a plan. They are either unaware or know full well that the act of homosexuality is part of a broader depopulation agenda. This European inspired eugenics tactic is one that has always been aimed at the black community.

Because, as science has shown us, it typically takes a healthy Wombman (woman) and man to create another human being. And this act is typically accomplished by way of the physical exchange of energy and emotion called sex. And as we all know, homosexuals do not reproduce.

And I am of the belief that diverting the public's attention away from critical matters is an unspoken job requirement of entertainers, athletes, and media personnel who are paid outrageous salaries, while the salaries of some of society's most vital positions such as teachers, nurses, and firemen pale drastically in comparison. And it is not as if these individuals are smarter or have special training.

No, to the contrary, they are being rewarded, knowingly or unknowingly, for their assistance in this slow takeover of humanity erroneously labeled a *new world order*. It is their duty to keep the masses entertained and diverted from the truth by any means necessary.

6

Violence

You can't talk about fucking in America; people say you're dirty. But if you talk about killing somebody, that's cool.

—RICHARD PRYOR

VIOLENCE IS NOT only a way of life for the European in America; it is a business—and a very prosperous business at that.

The pale-skin nations have used violence as a means to achieve any and everything they have desired. The matter of violently taking what you want simply because you can is at best barbaric, but the pale-skin nation has broken it down to a science. It's called *survival of the fittest.*

This is where any concept of social living is completely null and void. For whatever reason this may be, it appears that warmongering and violence seems to be the only way Europeans feel they can survive in a world and environment dominated by melanin or carbon.

How else would one explain that a country—or, shall I say, a *corporation*—the United States of America, which is only 240 years old, has been at war for 223 of those 240 years, and this has all taken place while not being attacked on its soil by a foreign military force a single time?

This US government has been at war 93 percent of the time since its inception. Are we to believe that a country that has never been without slaves is actually fighting to free people in a faraway land?

Are we to believe that they are freeing a people whose dark skin mirrors the slaves they so bitterly brutalized here in their own land? Do you really believe that?

No, of course, you don't.

The US military has bases in over 130 countries, over nine hundred bases totally around the world. It is involved in every major and minor military conflict on the globe and is also the biggest arms (weapons) dealer in the entire world, hands down.

The US government invests more money and resources to warmongering than other nations on the planet *combined*. The US Armed Forces are, far and away, the most destructive fighting force the world has ever known. They have taken part in illegal wars and occupations, CIA-planned coups, and the targeting of countries via economics or gunboat diplomacy.

You name it, if it is destroying the planet and killing large numbers of people of color in the process, it is highly probable that your government is involved in it some form or fashion. These endless waves upon waves of wars are not fought for the well-being of US citizens.

No!

Please remember that this government is really a corporation. These unnecessary imperial wars of aggression are only fought to serve and enrich a tiny few—the 1 percent. Yet they also serve a dual purpose as well, and that's to keep the people of color on the planet in check and under the thumbnail of the pale-skin nations.

If this government's unjustified wars and other evil actions don't muster up terrorists the organic way—you know, by bombing their innocent families—it creates them, just like it did with Al Qaeda and now ISIS.

Both of these terrorist organizations were created and hired to basically be mercenary fighting forces for the US government. By this I mean that the government will sic them on countries that balk at being down with central banking and this new-world-order idea.

Please believe me when I tell you this, loved ones: This is what is commonly referred to as an *empire*. The corporate-owned media have the civilian population of America believing that this violent, out-of-control corporation that is pretending to be government for the people and by the people is also a force for good in our world!

Believing such a notion is dangerously preposterous.

The making of war and the colonial footprint war leaves are not only a part of European culture. They have, in a lot of instances, become European culture, because war, according to former president George W. Bush, is a business—and a business that is doing quite well, with no apparent end in sight.

The business of war generates enormous monetary profits for corporations, which employ mainly European workers who are raking in very large salaries. This would certainly explain the power and influence the military industrial complex wields over the governing body of the United States.

The making of military hardware, to be used primarily as an offensive weapon to kill people of color, is run and operated by the pale-skin nations. The military industrial complex is an industry, and just like any other industry, it is always seeking to expand its sphere of influence. This is done in an effort to accumulate more wealth and power.

The ruling European nations have always used violence as means to obtain worldly resources and global power. Violence is so entrenched and indoctrinated into European American culture that it has now officially become American culture.

It seems as though if the white man cannot buy you off, he will then attempt to use his religion to control and subdue you. If, for whatever reason, that is not successful, they will then come for you with their Roman law.

Yet while all of this is transpiring, black people are busy entertaining or being entertained. Either way, it is preventing our community from seeing the real problem, which is usually right in front of our faces.

And last but never least, if *capitalism*, *religion*, *law*, and *entertainment* fail to achieve their planned result, the pale-skin nations will always reserve the right to use *violence* as a means to keep their people and community in the desired position of being on top.

So it should come as no surprise that the European has been making war and bombing countries the world over. This was done with one desired goal in mind, and that's the complete control over all the earth's resources, while enslaving much of humanity in the process.

From Cambodia to Africa to the Americas and the surrounding islands, an individual would be hard pressed to find a country or a region that has not been at war with the Europeans—if not at this present time, at least at some point in their respective histories.

Just about every crime against humanity has been committed by the minority European populace of the planet. This appears to be a deliberate act of systemic violence by the Europeans. So when the game changes little and the major players are the same, we know then that we are dealing with a violent system of oppression that lacks self-control.

If you do not believe me, just take a simple glance through history, and you will find that some of the most grievous crimes committed against the earth and her earthlings have been perpetrated by the Caucasoid nations.

What is even more troubling is the fact that the majority of pale-skins in America see absolutely nothing wrong with the violence that is being committed in their name and for their economic benefit. The police violence we are witnessing today in America and have historically seen being handed out to the so-called black and brown communities is really just a continuation of the Christian Black Codes of 1724 and the Jim Crow laws, with the *unwritten policy* of maintaining white superiority over what is perceived as its property.

That property is you, *corporate* chattel.

The unwritten policy that all the pale-skin nations adhere to is to never allow the Muurs (of America) to rise as a unified nation again. That policy is standard, domestic- and international-operational procedure when it concerns the Europeans and their dealings with Muurs/Africans.

But it is here domestically, in the United States of America, that blacks must shift their focus away from the KKK and the symbolic hood that has terrorized many a people of color in this country and realize that the only mask racism hides behind now is the *corporate* veil.

If the use of violence by the Europeans in America is seen as a means of keeping their slaves in check while also maintaining their preferred position on top, I guess my next question is what has changed?

When the European national was gunning you down with no fear of judicial retribution whatsoever in the past, what will make the black community think anything will be different in the future?

Absolutely nothing will be different, simply because the so-called African American continues to have no lawful or legal recourse in the face of this brutality. I cannot think of a better quote to summarize the violence that the European in America has inflicted on black people than the following from Harvard scholar Garikai Chengu, who states that "a lynching was a quintessential American public ritual that often took place in front of large crowds that sometimes numbered in the thousands." Also, Historian Mark Gado notes that, 'onlookers sometimes fired rifles and handguns hundreds of times into the corpse while people cheered and children played during the festivities."

Mr. Chengu goes on to state that "in 1899, the *Springfield Weekly* described a lynching by chronicling how the Negro was deprived of his ears, fingers and genital parts of his body. He pleaded pitifully for his life while the mutilation was going on...Before the body was cool, it was cut to pieces, and the bones crushed into small bits...The Negro's heart was cut into several pieces, as was also the liver...small pieces of bones went for 25 cents." [27]

The same violence the US government issues out on the international scale was first perfected here in the Americas.

Another violent example is the Black Wall Street massacre in Tulsa, Oklahoma. It has been reported that this happened with assistance of the 101st Army Airborne Division. It was this unit that conducted the aerial bombardment used against the black civilian population.

This was done at the behest of the US government.

---

27 Garikai Chengu, The Rise of African-American Police State, Global-Research.ca, May 4th, 2015.

That incident can easily be called a live-training bombing exercise, or practice run for future bombing campaigns, exactly like the other bombing of the MOVE housing complex in Philadelphia, Pennsylvania, in 1985. The mass killing of black people was not just isolated to Tulsa, Oklahoma, or Philadelphia, for that matter.

No, to the contrary, this violent pattern of killing masses of black people flourished nationwide and reached its murderous peak in the early twentieth century.

Although it happened several years before the invention of the nuclear bomb, I am 1,000 percent sure that if the US government had access to the nuclear weapon back then, it would have most certainly been used against the black or dark-skinned inhabitants of Black Wall Street and the city of Tulsa, Oklahoma.

Another example of mass killing of nonwhite people is the totally unnecessary atomic bombing of the island country of Japan. It is now a historical fact that toward the end of World War II, Japan was already in talks to surrender.

Let's see what General, who later became president, Dwight Eisenhower had to say about capitulation of the Japanese during the war: "The Japanese were ready to surrender and it wasn't necessary to hit them with that awful thing."[28]

But it was the US government that would reject the surrender offer just so that it could test its new weapon—the atomic bomb. All of this was done after the US government baited the Japanese into attacking Pearl Harbor by imposing a naval blockade of the island nation of Japan. President Roosevelt, who under orders, from the international banking cartel, wanted war—a war that much of the American public did not want.

There was no surprise attack for two reasons. First the US government had already cracked the Japanese military code months

28 Newsweek Staff, "Ike on Ike," *Newsweek*, November 11, 1963.

before. And secondly, the United States had begun to put in place a series of moves that baited the Japanese into a military conflict. This first move was on July 2, 1940. President Roosevelt signed the Export Control Act, which prohibited the sale of materials including oil to the nation of Japan. Then on July 26, 1941, the US government placed economic sanctions on Japan; both acts of embargo and economic sanctions under international law are considered an act of war.

The unwarranted disposal of two atomic bombs was meant to not only destroy Japan but also as a shot across the bow, or a warning, to the other nations, particularly Russia, and humanity in general. The message was that the US government—the hub of European racism—would not hesitate to kill hundreds of thousands of people to advance its evil agenda.

Now, as for the United States being a Christian nation, well, Nagasaki, one of the two cities hit by the bomb, was Japan's only Christian city.

One would think that with the carnage the pale-skins have brought to bear on people of color around the world, they would feel some sort of remorse and make some serious inroads to repair the damage their community has done. That honestly has never happened, and I don't see it happening in the near future.

Shockingly it has been quite the opposite. As we have come to see from the pale-skins in America, they celebrate their warmongering accomplishments in movies, television, sport, and song. Warmongering is basically a part of so-called white American life, which includes this obscene and grotesque need to hunt and kill innocent animals for sport—not for food—all while their refrigerators are full to capacity with other animals that died in a similar fashion, most likely straight from the local slaughterhouse.

When I say that the European national is the apex predator of the human family, I mean no disrespect, but that statement is quite accurate and true. It is the pale-skin nations' insatiable thirst for war and capital gain that is the greatest threat to our planet and its inhabitants, yet this thirst is only satisfied by the unsanctioned killing of humans for their natural resources.

This celebratory energy also includes the use of music to glorify the Europeans' past military endeavors. How many of you remember hearing the US Marine fighting song? It is called the "Marines' Hymn," and it is the oldest official military song in US history.

Many of you may recognize it from the opening lines. Here's a snippet:

From the Halls of Montezuma
To the shores of Tripoli,
We fight our country's battles,
In the air, on land, and sea.

It's a very catchy hymn on face value, but let us a take deeper look at the song and see what the lyrics are really telling us. We know from real and true history that the Aztec leader Motecuhzoma was in the Americas, specifically Mexico.

In the "Marines' Hymn," the US Marines were fighting on the shores of Tripoli in North Africa as well. Will it shock you to learn that Mexico and Tripoli were at one time considered Moor territory?

I find that to be very interesting because the US Marines were fighting one enemy but on the two completely different continents of America and Africa. I also find this interesting because that military expedition to North Africa, or Tripoli, was the first time that US Marines were in combat outside of the landmass called the America(s).

The lyrics to the "Marines' Hymn" were written by a young marine fighting in Mexico, and the lyrics to the song can be traced back to the nineteenth century.

Horace Butler in his book *When Rocks Cry Out* references *The Letters of Cortes* by Hernando Cortes, the leader of the Spanish Christian invasion of Mexico.

In the letter, it describes the war with the Aztecs (Muurs) as well as the physical appearance of the Aztecs, including their famous leader named Motecuhzoma. It also states that the Aztec leader Motecuhzoma himself told Hernando Cortes directly that his ancestors are not the aboriginals of Mexico.

Again this is extremely interesting because his statement was made while he, Motecuhzoma, was in Mexico. The book goes on to say that the Aztecs came to Mexico on ships from the direction where the sun rises, which is east from the direction of Africa.

Let us take a look at another particular passage from *When Rocks Cry Out*. It details who the Aztecs encountered and how those who were encountered appeared. "The illustration was published in 1724 on a front page of Antonio de Solis' History of the Conquest of Mexico. The artist had allowed the buildings in the illustration to be Moorish in design, and he had allowed all but one of the Aztecs to be black-skinned. He, or someone, had lightened, considerably, the complexion of Motecuhzoma."[29]

This account of the carnage inflicted on the Aztecs by Cortes and his troops lends further support to what other Spanish historians and writers knew about the early inhabitants of the Americas, particularly Mexico.

Indeed it was Cortez's very own secretary as well as one of his officers that described Motecuhzoma and the Aztecs as "being

29 Horace Butler, When Rocks Cry Out, Nashville, 2009, p.60.

very dark complexioned. They wrote that the nation of people they found here was of the same complexion."[30]

Real history has also shown us that Motecuhzoma spoke an early form of the Muhammadan language, or what is called Arabic. Motecuhzoma himself was described by the Spanish invaders as a small-framed man with a very dark skin tone.

Also, as a bit of a side note, there are businesses in Los Angeles, California, and towns in Mexico that are named Matamoros, which, when translated from Spanish to English, means a "killer of Moors/Muurs."

The African/Muur ancestry of the Aztecs and the Mayans should come as no surprise, considering that they both are direct descendants of the Xi people or the Olmecs.

I have seen the picture of the Mayans from a *National Geographic* commemorative magazine issue. The issue includes many pictures and one in particular was a self-portrait that the Mayans had painted. The reader can clearly see the difference between the artist's renditions of the Mayans and the way that the Mayans actually portrayed themselves.

The picture is in color, and it shows, beyond any doubt, the Mayans to be a very dark-and/or-brown-skin– complexioned people sporting the dreadlock hairstyle. Now when one sees the self-portrayal of the Mayans and then takes a look at the artist's rendition of the same people, the artist's intentions becomes very clear.

That is, to continue with plan A: concealment.

All artists' portrayals of the Mayans make them out to be native Indians or, as European history will have you believe, early Mexicans. This of course is nicely done to fit right in line with the system and its web of lies. The major problem with this theory—if

30 Horace Butler, When Rocks Cry Out, Nashville, 2009, p.65.

one can even call it a theory—is that the Xi people, misnamed the Olmecs, were and are a negroid or Muur/African race of people and that all of humanity, including the Aztecs and the Mayans, descend from them.

I personally find that individuals from other nationalities do not have a problem accepting the prevalent and readily accepted slave story conveniently used to explain our (Muurs) presence in the Americas. But these people get absolutely upset at any mention of Muurs being in the Western Hemisphere before the Indians and Europeans.

So, the next time you hear the "Marines' Hymn" or someone speaking about it or the next time you see a US Marines commercial—and you will—you should have a better overstanding of the song and the organization it represents.

Once again, according to the oldest US military song, the marines were fighting from the Halls of Motecuhzoma (Mexico) to the shores of Tripoli (North Africa). This is very critical information because the only *world* empire to have ever existed that was comprised of people with very dark complexion was that of the Muurs/Muurs.

At its height and strength, the ancient Muur Empire was located here in the Americas. To be exact, it was North America in the Bey, or Bay, Area of California, and it literally stretched worldwide.

This history, of course, was supposed to be gone forever because any mention of a Muur/African presence in the early Americas, pre-Columbus or pre-Indians is strictly forbidden in any European-dominated society, especially in historical and academic circles.

The foreign European nationals had what was called a *reconstruction period* on this land after the war with the Moors/Muurs. That is when they attempted to write the Muurs out of history forever. But history is now revealing its secrets.

In the book, *The Black West,* William Katz quotes General Thomas Jessup saying, "This, you may be assured, is a Negro, not an Indian war, and if it be speedily put down, the south will feel the effects of it on their slave population before the end of the next season."

The book also quotes him as saying, "Throughout my operations I found the 'Negroes' the most active and determined warriors; and during the conferences with the 'Indian' chiefs, I ascertained they exercised an almost controlling influence over them...The 'Negroes' rule the Indian."[31]

Also according to the book *Biography of the Moors,* by Claudus M. El, the War of 1812 is where the Muurs suffered their final defeat at the hands of the invading European forces. Mr. El writes,

"The last of the Moorish armies was located in the Midwest. The armies were led by Sheik T. Compre Bey. The European armies met Bey and his forces at the Midwest in one of the most bloodiest and longest battles ever fought in America. It became known as the battle of 1812.

T. Compre Bey and his Moorish armies went down with the Moorish flag in that great battle. The Europeans named the area where the battle took place Battle Creek, Michigan".[32]

Furthermore from this battle we have learned that as part of the so-called blacks buried oral history. That the surviving Muur soldiers and orphans were forced to brutally walk down South for enslavement; this is where the Europeans would later raise the orphans as Negros, blacks, and colored, stripping them of their noble titles (El, Bey, Ali) and history for generations to come.

31 William Katz, The Black West, New York, Touchstone, 2005, p.18
32 Claudus M. El, *Biography of the Moors,* New York: R.V.Bey Publications, 2015), p.8.

Let us never forget that the victor of wars always rewrites the history of the people just conquered.

The war that was fought between the Muurs and Christian powers was just an extension of the early Crusades and the Barbary Wars. This is why there exists an international treaty between the Muurs and the Christian powers—or the US government. It will also explain why this treaty just happens to be the oldest unbroken treaty in US history. It is called the Treaty of Peace and Friendship.

It remains unbroken in part due to it not being enforced. Enforcing said treaty is quite difficult to do when the people written into the treaty are known as Muurs, but their descendants have since been denationalized and now joyfully refer to themselves as an adjective—*black*.

Barack Obama states in *Dreams from My Father: A Story of Race and Inheritance,* "The worst thing that colonialism did was to cloud our view of our past."[33]

We have familiarized ourselves with the Europeans' past and present violent military conquest here and abroad. It is here in the United States of America that only the so-called black people can bear witness to his brutality on this said land, which was and is being perpetrated by the regular, ordinary white citizen.

We all know that slavery, the violent cousin of war, was hyper cruel and unusual, but the slave laws that came later were not much better. Yet from slavery to the KKK and the slave patrols to the modern-day police force, it appears that historically—and even up until this present time—the pale-skin nation in America has always had some form of system supported by color of laws and violence, whose only purpose is to keep its black population in check.

---

33 Barack Obama. Dreams from My Father: A Story of Race and Inheritance, New York, Crown Publishing Group, p.434,

The use of violence is a matter of business as usual for much of white America in this country. With every problem this society faces, the pale-skin nation feels the need to solve the problem via war. The use of war to solve issues that normally would have never thought to be solved by violence is now common in this society.

A few examples of this are the following: problems with poverty (now enter the War on Poverty) and problems with drug use (enter the War on Drugs). Any and every societal obstacle that plagues this commonwealth is settled by the notion of war.

The ruling European powers feel the need to solve the issue by force—not literally but mentally. You get the point.

During the business of slave catching, the owners kept encountering the problem of slaves who had this weird knack of running or escaping in an all-out effort to obtain their God-given right to be free. The black community should be more than aware of the historical fact that today's modern police force has its origins in the white European American slave patrols, freemasonry, and the KKK.

The Europeans in America devised and created legal organizations that caught and returned, at times, any slave who had run away. According to a study titled *A Brief History of Slavery and the Origins of American Policing* conducted by Eastern Kentucky University, "It was the year of 1704 in the colony of Carolina that saw the development of the nation's first slave patrol. Slave patrols helped to maintain the economic order and to assist the wealthy landowners in recovering and punishing slaves who essentially were considered property."[34]

A blind man can see that it was official policy that for economic and safety reasons alone, *all* slaves who ran had to be returned to the rightful owner. These newly created slave laws were not confined to the south. No, they flourished nationwide.

---

34 Victor E. Kappeler, Eastern Kentucky University, Online Study of Slavery and American History of Policing, 2015.

Real history in America has clearly shown us that the first law-enforcement system was indeed a system of catch and return that involved any slave who escaped seeking his or her own freedom. This slave-enforcement system, with its masonic KKK origins, would later become the modern police force we see patrolling the streets of America today.

So it should come as no surprise that the police force in America is really the policy enforcer for the wealthy. That statement most certainly rings true now.

You see, the descendants of the wealthy European slave owners of the past are also the owners of the highly successful private-prison industry we see in America today. This system, as we currently know it, has made the warehousing of humans into a big business industry simply because it is policy that those correctional facilities must be filled to maintain certain prisoner quotas.

As it relates to police brutality, there is one crucial aspect I would like my community to inner-, under-, and overstand: the police force we see patrolling our streets today is without a shadow of doubt the *first-line defenders of global white supremacy.*

To ensure that the police force of America is properly trained in the art of brutalizing an entire nation of people, they are being trained by the very best the world has to offer in the art of oppression, and that would be the totally rogue state of Israel.

There are some who say that the Israeli government has South Africa, India, and, of course, the United States beat in regard to it being a violent, racist society. Much of humanity has had a front-row seat to see how the abusive apartheid regime of Israel deals with their neighbors, the Palestinians.

Yet the world just sits and continues to do absolutely nothing to help the Palestinians and their awful living conditions. The unimaginable horrors inflicted on the Palestinian people are heart wrenching, yet this is where the US government sends its *community* police to be trained?

A police force that was born out of slavery and racism will only grow to become a larger and more powerful police force that is born out of slavery and racism.

The police just added a little color, and became ultraviolent, yet now they are trained in terrorist tactics by the most despicable country on the planet. With that being the case, still a large majority of our community act surprised at the level of violence directed at its nonwhite populace by its local police departments.

When the police in America were directing much of their violence at people of color, it was widely considered by much of white America to be good policing. But when the police put their hands on a few white folk, now the society we domicile in is an out-of-control police state!

You don't say.

Maybe for white folk, it is *now* a police state, but for those with melanin in this country, it has always been government policy to oppress and exploit the melaninated people of this society by any means necessary, up to and including the unmitigated use of violence.

Conclusion

Proposed Remedy

Analyzing obstacles and intelligently overcoming them.

—Vaughn Benjamin of the reggae band Midnite

A s I write this, there is a generation of so-called black people who are experiencing racism in America, the likes of
which they have never seen before. It honestly looks like all the
work that had been done during the pre– and post–civil rights
era has all been for naught.

It pains me to admit this, but those past struggles have produced no results—absolutely nothing in the way of our dealings
with the ever-increasing problem of racism.

I would like to think that after reading this book our community can now be armed with the overstanding that if the African
American community had knowledge of nationality and statehood

during the civil rights era and proclaimed their nationality as a unified nation, the "civil" rights movement would be unnecessary and nonexistent. That's because, as a nation, our fight will always be on the human level and for human rights.

Yet after all the marches and the sit-ins, the civil rights movement, the rise and fall of the Black Panther Party, the countless economic boycotts, and the proposed black economic forums, now add to the list the heartfelt but terribly misguided Black Lives Matter movement.

Listen, if you repeatedly have to tell your known oppressor in 2017 that your black life matters, as if black lives mattered in 1917, and we know black lives didn't matter during that said time, our community should really rethink its approach to these people whom you are now begging to treat you right. These are the very people whom you so affectionately call *white*, which, by definition, means angelic, pure, and good.

To top it off, the black community had an African American as a president, with countless senators and house representatives who are also with melanin, and these politicians are a major part of the problem—not a solution for our community.

The so-called African in America has unknowingly and knowingly accepted the Europeans' form of God consciousness, their culture, their diet, and their ways—all by simply volunteering to do so. By doing this, our community has usurped our very own social structure for the pale-skins' way of life, all with disastrous consequences.

The European's so-called holidays are celebrated in full by people of color in this country. This is done even when those very celebrations are nothing more than a joyous embrace of a violent colonial past and, at times, involve our very own ancestors as the victims. If an individual does not know his true history, the pale-skin holidays can be a moment of jubilee for that person and his family, and yet through it all, so-called black people are still directly in the crosshairs of European racism.

How many times must families of color receive roadside justice at the hands of bigoted cops who are working in unison with a racist judicial system?

If it appears to some that racism, the *protector of global white supremacy*, is getting worse, that's because it *is* getting worse. And it will continue to do so until the black community wakes from its slumber, nationalizes, and begins the slow but necessary process of governing itself.

Again.

That, my friend, is the beauty of racism.

We know where racism is coming from and why it is upon us, yet we have not a clue as to how to properly and effectively deal with it. Be mindful that the issue of dealing with racism is not going to just fade away.

To my community, I say this with the upmost confidence: What we know as racism is not our only problem. This thing called racism also plays the role of the distractor, a diversion to keep you and those like you away from the simple matters of nationality and status.

It is our collective misunderstanding of the word *racism* and the international impact of global white supremacy that has led us to believe that this oppressive issue of race alone is the only problem confronting us. It's as if black people think that one glorious day, the pale-skins are going to wake up and apologize and then return the lands they have stolen and dominated over the years and repair the damage they have inflicted on you.

That has never happened in the history of humanity residing on this planet, and the likelihood that it will happen is an impossibility. It is the ancient past that demonstrates what happens to the oppressor and the oppressed.

The blueprint we need has been shown and proven historically that when a race of people is faced with a foreign oppressor—in this case, the Europeans are just that—those oppressed people will *nationalize* and *unite* to defeat the threat at any and all costs, regardless of any individual's religious belief and/or personal feelings.

Let us take a quick glance again at the oldest known definition of the noun *Muur/Moor.* It is defined as "all the dark-skin people on the planet, *especially* Negroes."[35]

Why, again?

I repeated this again because there is unity in the very definition of the word. We all have dark skin, and we all are dealing with the same issue of racism.

In the Bible it is written that my people are destroyed for lack of knowledge. I say this because as a community who self-identifies itself as *black*, an adjective, and that brand is interpreted by the ruling pale-skin government as a people with no nationality.

As we covered in chapter 2, that label makes the so-called black people in America effectively wards of the bankrupt state, or slaves. This again is no accident.

Some will go as far to say it's a masonic secret, one I personally believe to be true, because that accusation will be in conjunction with just about all US politicians—including presidents, senators, House representatives, judges, lawyers, and all major CEOs—who by coincidence are freemasons also.

The connections between freemasonry, this US government, and your Muur nationality are very historic, secretive, and immense. It is no accident as to why you will never hear these two words together in this country: *African American* and *nationality.* You cannot mention those two in relation with one another

---

35 Webster's Third New International Dictionary

because your nationality, which is *Muur American*, ties you directly to this landmass called the America(s).

Your problem is that you do not know this.

The powers that be also know that African Americans as a people have no cultural connections to the continent of Africa. The Vatican, in partnership with the so-called Illuminati, is also very aware of this.

The pale-skin freemasons who now run the government are very mindful of the enormous debt that is owed to the Muurs and also the power the Muurs can wield as a nation. As a nation of Muurs, we will have again the power to send the Europeans back to their homeland and repair our community and the planet; all while being backed by the international community and, in large part, the entire world.

I remember being told by an elder that when the Muurs stood as a once proud and powerful empire, no one on the planet starved. Our societies were mostly matriarchal communities, where man, woman, and child acted as one with nature and fellow beings, because we recognized the bounty that our environment provided as it relates to our earthly sustenance.

The days of so-called black people depending on white America to provide jobs, health care, housing, and access to healthy food choices are fast becoming a distant memory. And they should. Because the fact of the matter is that the pale-skin nation has more than failed in its attempts to provide said things to people whom it perceives as its property.

This is why change is so desperately required.

To bring about our desired change, an *in-the-hood or grassroots national movement* must take place in order for us as a community to regain our lofty estate. This change has already begun to take place, because Muurs like me have proclaimed our *individual n*ationality on public record with all governmental and corporate agencies.

For the so-called black community to get released from the clutches of racism, we must separate and form our own nation on this land. Our problems stem from the lack of overstanding of our true national status as Muurs/Moors. And because of this, we find ourselves getting all wrapped up in this smoke screen called racism, playing the crayon game that only benefits Europeans.

The European chose to be *white* and assigned *black* to you.

We have unknowingly let the pale-skin nations take us down to their low vibrational level by attempting to coexist with a people with whom no one can coexist peacefully. I liken it to ramming your head into a brick wall and then starting to complain to the brick wall of headaches.

It is you, the so-called black people, who in your *arrogance of ignorance* have to shoulder a lot of the blame when it comes to your dependence on this system of exploitation, because the black community as a collective unit portray themselves as if they need this pale skin. That literally and personally bothers the hell out of this writer.

Our community seems as if it is unwilling to or incapable of properly governing themselves, and the pale-skin nation now has the job of determining what is good and bad for us. And that, my friend, is the source of our problems right there.

Here's a simple example.

Let's say that you do not personally care for a certain individual. You really don't like that person at all and may even harbor some jealousy toward the person, even hatred at times. But amid all those ill feelings toward that individual, you are tasked to provide food, clothing, and shelter for the very person you so bitterly despise. The question then becomes, would that person receive the best possible treatment from you?

Now are we really surprised at the treatment we receive as a nationless community from the ruling pale-skin authorities?

The descendants of the cavemen and or the Neanderthals are now governing over the descendants of the mothers and fathers of human civilization with terrible results. And this is done with the unconscious Muurs of America appearing completely bewildered as to how to change this devastating cycle.

This necessary change will have to take place at the local level. It has to do so because our so-called black leaders are an embarrassment to us as a people, and they have completely sold out their respective communities.

And it is not just a few of them. It is all of them.

If a black man or woman just happens to be in some type of leadership position within our community or government and routinely speaks on the conditions of our people but never mentions the words *nationality* (Muurs) and *governing of self,* I question any and everything about those people and their cause. Thus I cannot support it and will warn others against it.

Until we nationalize and *remember* how to govern ourselves, we will continue to be treated as second-class citizens, as this treatment now plays out on the world stage, thanks to the media.

There is a crucial need for us to begin this transition back into a nation again. Our very survival as a people depends on it, because all men, women, and children in the very near future must return to their indigenous land of origin. And since African Americans at this current time are unaware of their national name and origin, this leaves the US government scrambling to find out what to do with their *corporate property.*

This is transpiring as we make our way through the age of nations. While doing so, we are also witnessing the fall of the European model of government known as the corporate state.

This is the bankrupt form of government that has enslaved much of humanity and is gradually destroying our beautiful planet.

We also know that the US federal government was dissolved by the Emergency Banking Act declared by President Roosevelt on March 9, 1933. What was left in its place is a shell of a company, which is insolvent and has been in chapter-11 bankruptcy status since 1933.

This is the same corporation that also views the US citizen as commercial property to do with as it pleases, up to and including the introduction of liquidation facilities also known as FEMA or internment camps. There is a mountain of evidence to back up my FEMA-camp statement, yet ones&ones do not believe that this is possible.[36]

Do you believe that the European would never do such a thing?

If you are so naïve as to believe that this is not possible after all they've done historically, then there is not too much I or anyone can do or say to help you.

Good luck.

As for those of us who are familiar with the pale-skins' past violence, we may also be privy to their future plans, which happen to involve more acts of violence.

Enter now the diabolical King Alfred Plan.

The King Alfred Plan was developed in the 1960s by the National Security Council of the US government. This plan explained in great detail the proposed encampment and extermination of the black and Hispanic communities of America.

Allow me to make you aware that this plan would also include the government seeking assistance in the roundup of blacks and Hispanics from the KKK and any other white-supremacist

---

36 See United States House Resolution 645 and United States House Resolution 390.

organizations willing to help. It will be through the usage of bla-tant racism, violence, and greed that the pale-skins set the table for civil unrest to envelop much of this society.

This plan has purposely been put in motion by those who run your "government," with them knowing full well that, at some point, even a rat will abandon a sinking ship. The sinking ship in this example will be the bankrupt corporation that is pretending to be the US government.

The evil ones in charge of your government operate as follows:

1. They create the problem.
2. They gauge the reaction of the populace.
3. They come forth with the preplanned, desired solution.

The problem has already been created. They have been gauging your reactions for quite some time now, and the King Alfred Plan is their idea of a desired solution.

All of this will all be done under the guise of security and safety.

I came in love and now will depart you in peace.

Salaam.

BIBLIOGRAPHY

Alexander, Michelle. *The New Jim Crow: Mass Incarceration in the Age of Colorblindness.* New York: The New Press, 2012.

Ali, Sharif. "Ancient Moors in America: We Didn't Land on Plymouth Rock." www.moorsinaamerica.com

Aquinas, Thomas. *Summa Theologica.* Cincinnati, OH: Benziger Bros, 1947.

Ayana, R. "The Eighteen Most Suppressed Inventions." New Illuminati. www.nexusilluminati.blogspot.com.

Barton, Paul A. "The Olmecs: An African Presence in Early America." www.essaysbyekowa/olmecs.

Bey, Alim. "The Official United Washitaw De Dugdahmoundyah Muur Nation History." www.dralimelbey.com.

Bishop, Vic. "The Illusion of Choice: Ninety Percent of American Media Controlled by Six Corporations." Waking Times, August 28th, 2015. www.globalresearch.ca.

Black, Henry Campbell. *Black's Law Dictionary.* Eagan, MN: West Publishing, 1968.

Butler, Horace. *When Rocks Cry Out.* Conroe, TX: Stone River Publishing, 2009.

Claudus M. El. *Biography of the Moors.* New York: R.V. Bey Publications, 2015.

Cornell University Law School. "US Constitution." www.law.cornell.edu/constitution.

Cortes, Hernan. *The Letters from Mexico.* New Haven, CT: Yale University Press, 2001.

Deschesne, David. "Structure of the Birth Certificate: Did the State Pledge Your Body to a Bank?" Advanced Civics Research Library. www.jesus-is-savior.com.

Diop, Cheikh Anta. *The African Origin of Civilization: Myth or Reality.* Chicago, IL: Chicago Review Press, 1989.

Eastern Kentucky University Police Studies Online. "A Brief History of Slavery and the Origins of American Policing." January 7, 2014. www.plsonline.eku.edu/insidelook/brief-history-slavery-and-origins-american-policing.

El, Tauheedah N., and Victor Taylor El. *Moors in America: A Compilation.* Riverdale, IL: Califa Media, 2014.

Expose. 1993. "Your Name in Capital Letters Exposed." www.expose1933.com.

Forbes, Jack D. *Africans and Native Americans: The Language of Race and the Evolution of the Red-Black Peoples.* Champaign, IL: University of Illinois Press, 1993.

Gowans, Stephen. "Aspiring to Rule the World: US Capitalism and the Battle for Syria What's Left." Centre for Research on Globalization, November 30, 2015. http://www.globalresearch.ca/aspiring-to-rule-the-world-us-capitalism-and-the-battle-for-syria/5492433.

Griffin, G. Edward. *The Creature from Jekyll Island: A Second Look at the Federal Reserve, New York*, American Media, 1998.

Imhotep, David. *The First Americans Were African: Documented Evidence.* Bloomington, IN: AuthorHouse, 2011.

Israel, Hebrew. "The Physical Appearance of Ancient Israel the Hebrews and the Sons of Ham." www.angelfire.com Israel/ printpages/phys.html.

James, George G. M. *Stolen Legacy: The Egyptian Origins of Western Philosophy.* North Charleston, SC: CreateSpace, 2014.

Jaspin, Elliot G. *Buried in Bitter Waters: The Hidden History of Racial Cleansing in America.* New York: Basic Books, 2008.

Judge Dale. "The Great American Adventure: Secrets of America." AntiCorruption Society. www.anticorruptionsociety.files.wordpress.com.

Kangas, Steve. "A Timeline of CIA Atrocities." Huppi. http://www. huppi.com/kangaroo/CIAtimeline.html.

Katz, William Loren. *The Black West: A Documentary and Pictorial History of the African American Role in the Westward Expansion of the United States.* New York: Touchstone, 1996.

Lost Feather. "Black Seminoles." http://lostfeather.weebly.com/ black-seminoles.html.

Muhammad, Elijah. "The Real Indian Is the Negro a.k.a. the Blackamoor." Mamiwata. www.mamiwata.com/Moors.pdf.

Muhammad, Wesley. "Black Arabia and the African Origin of Islam." Black Arabia. www.blackarabia.blogspot.com.

Myers-EL, Noble Timothy. *The Huevolution of Sacred Muur Science Past and Present: A Theoretical Compilation.* Bloomington, IN: AuthorHouse, 2004.

National Center for Biotechnology Information. "Cannabis Inhibits Cancer Cells." www.ncbi.nlm.nih.gov.

National Geographic Proves Teaching on Mr. Yakub article, May 23, 2013. www.finalcall.com.

Obama, Barack. *Dreams from My Father: A Story of Race and Inheritance.* New York: Broadway Books, 2004.

Pimienta-Bey, Jose V. "Muslim Legacy in Early Americas, West African, Moors, and Amerindians." 2013. www.cyberistan.org/ilamic/africanm.htm.

Pleasant-Bey, Elihu N. *Noble Drew Ali: The Exhuming of a Nation.* New York: Seven Seals Publication, 2009.

Reading Religion. "Christianity and Slavery." www.worldfuture.org.

Robinson, David E. *Give Yourself Credit.* North Charleston, SC: CreateSpace, 2010.

Sertima, Ivan Van. *They Came Before Columbus: The African Presence in Ancient America.* New York: Random House Trade Paperbacks, 2003.

Street, Paul. "False Flag: History, the Confederate Flag, Obama and the Deeper American Racism." Counterpunch.org, July 10, 2015.

Tarik Bey, Taj. *What to Study? Motecuhzoma.* Online Publications. rvbeypublications.com.

The Avalon Project. "The Barbary Treaties 1786–1816: The Treaty of Peace and Friendship." avalon.law.yale.edu/18th_century/bar1786t.asp.

The Real History of White People. "Ancient Man and His First Civilizations." www.realhistory.com.

Chang, Pao, "The Vatican (2015)—The Greatest Usurper Enslaving All of Humanity." May 3, 2017 www.omnithought.org

Waduge, Shenali D. "Three Corporations Run the World: City of London, Washington, DC, and Vatican City." Sinhalanet, May 31, 2014. www.sinhalanet.net.

Washington's Blog. "The Real Reason America Used Nuclear Weapons Against Japan (It Was Not to End the War or to Save Lives)." October 14, 2012. http://www.washingtonsblog.com/2012/10/the-real-reason-america-used-nuclear-weapons-against-japan-to-contain-russian-ambitions.html.

Windsor, Rudolph R. *From Babylon to Timbuktu: A History of the Ancient Black Races Including the Black Hebrews.* Atlanta, GA: Windsor Golden Series, 1969.

You Are the Law. "The Birth Certificate Power." www.youarelaw.org.

Zoubeir, Hisham. "Islam in America before Columbus." Islam the Modern Religion, February 14, 1998. www.themodernreligion. com.

About the Author

AZIZ BEY GREW up in South Central Los Angeles. Surrounded by gang violence, he found a safe space at home, buoyed by his love for reading, writing, and dreaming. His father's strong presence in his life helped guide him to adulthood, and conversations with his mother about South African apartheid helped him look honestly at racism in America.